THE SNOWMAN™
in Cross Stitch

FOR NIGEL

THE SNOWMAN™
in Cross Stitch

by Leslie Norah Hills

MURDOCH
B O O K S

Contents

Projects

Introduction

Adults and children alike are captivated by the story of the loveable Snowman who comes to life and takes a little boy on a fantastic night-time adventure. Raymond Briggs' thrilling tale has been made into a popular animated film and his beautifully illustrated books are perennial favourites. I have been designing Snowman cross stitch kits for two years now, and the idea for this book came about because people kept asking me if they could buy the charts on their own. I have arranged the designs to follow the story of the Snowman, from the very beginning when James realizes that it's snowing and runs outside to make a snowman, through to the end when he is left wondering if he has dreamed the whole of the intervening adventure.

The story is told in panels and these are interspersed with projects that continue the Snowman theme. The designs are not difficult to complete and most are well within the scope of a beginner. If you are not yet confident of your cross stitch skills, choose designs that don't incorporate fractional stitches or much back stitch. Those who are more confident could have fun adapting these designs for other projects, such as Christmas cushion covers and Snowman bedspreads. Many of the designs that accompany the projects can be used simply as attractive pictures.

Most designs use threads and fabrics of similar colours, and they can be interchanged. DMC threads are used throughout the book, and the nearest equivalent Anchor shade is also given in the keys. Please note that the Anchor colours are not exact replacements for the DMC ones and may give a slightly different effect.

I hope that this book will give people countless hours of pleasure and that it will reward the reader with many attractive items to treasure.

Leslie Norah Hills

It's Snowing!

Like all young boys, James was delighted when he awoke to find that it was snowing and couldn't wait to rush outside to play in the snow. As yet, he had no idea of the magic of The Snowman and the adventures that awaited him.

You will need

- 14 count Aida in white, 36 x 33cm (14 x 13in)
- Stranded embroidery thread as given in the key
- No. 24 tapestry needle
- Strong card
- Strong thread for lacing
- Mount and frame of your choice

FINISHED DESIGN SIZE
15 x 13.5cm (6 x 5¼in)

STITCHING THE PANEL

1 Cut out the fabric, leaving enough excess to form a border around the design and use an embroidery frame. The amount suggested will give approximately 5–7.5cm (2–3in) of unstitched fabric all round the design.

2 Prepare the fabric as instructed on page 104. Bind the edges with masking tape to prevent them from fraying. Find the centre of your fabric by folding it in half from top to bottom, then again from left to right, and mark it with a pin or thread.

3 Find the centre of the chart and mark it for your reference. Work with two strands of embroidery thread in your needle and begin stitching your design from this central point. Each cross stitch is worked across one square of the fabric, and you should ensure that all the top stitches follow the same direction and are neat and tidy.

4 Use Grey 414 for the back stitch around the figure. For the eyebrows and hair, use Orange 721. For the detail on the mouth, boots and jeans, use Black 310. Refer to the chart and key constantly to complete the cross stitching, remembering that each square of the chart represents one stitch.

5 Use silver thread for the snowflakes. Don't worry if your thread splits, as this will enhance the sparkly look of the design.

FINISHING THE PANEL

6 When the stitching is complete, you can remove your finished embroidery from the frame or hoop and hand wash it carefully in warm water. Then, lay the embroidery face down on a towel and press it gently with a warm iron until it is completely dry.

7 Choose a frame for the embroidery. Cut a piece of card to fit into the back of the frame and stretch the embroidery over it, as explained on pages 106–7.

8 Choose a mount that accentuates one of the least-used colours in the design. Assemble the glass (if desired), the mount and the embroidery in the frame and tape the backing board in place.

IT'S SNOWING!

		DMC	Anchor
O	Dark pink	224	893
−	Light pink	225	1026
■	Black	310	403
S	Grey	414	235
X	Dark yellow	725	305
I	Light blue	809	130
▽	Light yellow	3078	292
●	Dark red	3687	68
N	Light red	3712	1023
H	Dark blue	3807	122
◻	Orange	721	324
◻	Silver	ART 281	KBF

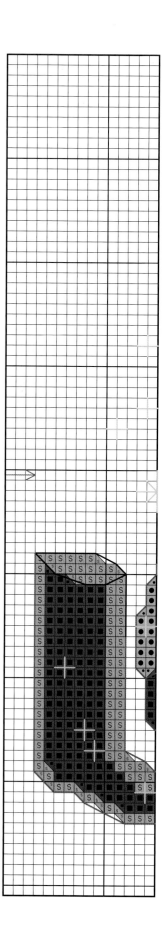

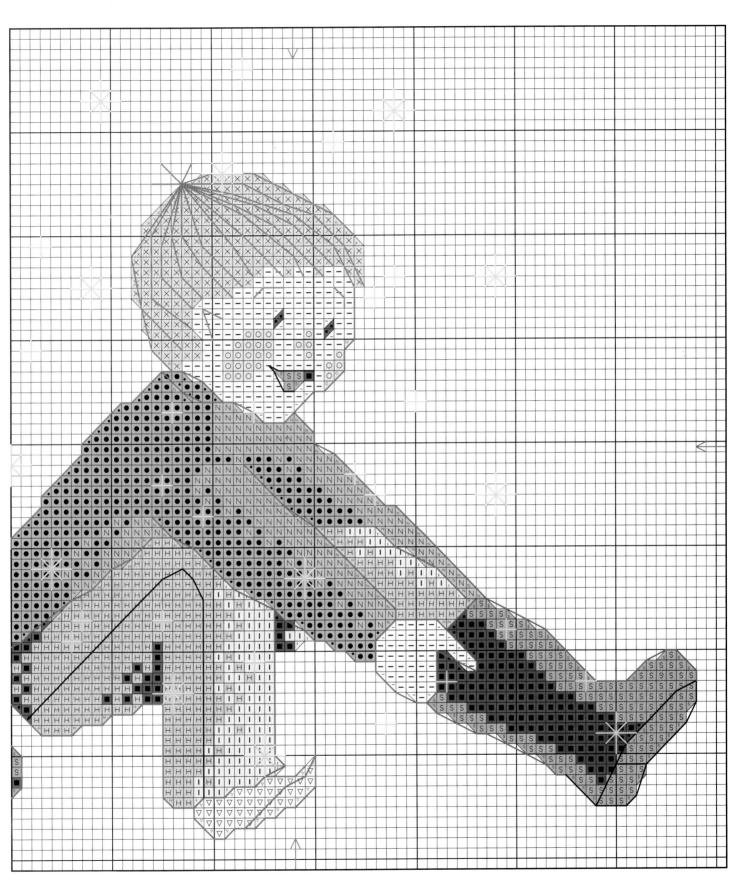

James Builds The Snowman

James's Snowman had grown so much that he had to use a
stool to complete him! He used a tangerine for The Snowman's
nose and lumps of coal for his buttons and eyes.

You will need

- 14 count Aida in light blue,
  33 x 46cm (13 x 18in)
- Stranded embroidery thread as given in the key
- No. 24 tapestry needle
- Strong card
- Strong thread for lacing
- Mount and frame of your choice

FINISHED DESIGN SIZE

13 x 23.5cm (5 x 9¹/4in)

STITCHING THE PANEL

1 Cut out the fabric, leaving enough excess to
form a border around the design and use an
embroidery frame. The amount suggested will give
approximately 5–7.5cm (2–3in) extra fabric.

2 Prepare the fabric as instructed on page 104.
Bind the edges with masking tape to prevent
them from fraying while you are working. Find the
centre of the fabric and mark it with a pin or
thread. You will start stitching here.

3 Find the centre of the chart and mark it for reference. Work with two strands of embroidery thread in your needle and begin stitching your design from this central point. Each cross stitch is worked over one square of the fabric. To achieve a neat-looking finish, you should ensure that all the top stitches run in the same direction.

4 Refer to the chart and key constantly to complete the cross stitching, remembering that each square of the chart represents one stitch. Use two strands of Grey 645 for the back stitch details, as indicated on the chart.

FINISHING THE PANEL

5 Your embroidery may have become a bit grubby as you worked on it so it is a good idea to hand wash it in warm water before you frame it. To dry the embroidery, lay it face down on a towel and press it gently with a warm iron.

6 Choose a frame for the embroidery. Cut a piece of card to fit into the back of the frame and stretch the embroidery over it, as explained on pages 106–7.

7 Choose a mount that accentuates one of the least-used colours in the design – perhaps the orange of The Snowman's nose or the dark green of his scarf. The colour you choose will be highlighted in the design. Assemble the glass (if desired), the mount and the embroidery in the frame and tape the backing board in place.

JAMES BUILDS THE SNOWMAN

		DMC	Anchor
·	White	blanc	2
O	Dark pink	224	893
−	Light pink	225	1026
■	Black	310	403
↑	Red	355	1014
T	Light green	470	267
△	Beige	612	832
□	Grey	645	273
Z	Orange	721	324
X	Yellow	725	305
I	Light blue	809	130
▲	Brown	869	944
●	Dark green	937	268
N	Light red	3712	1023
H	Dark blue	3807	122

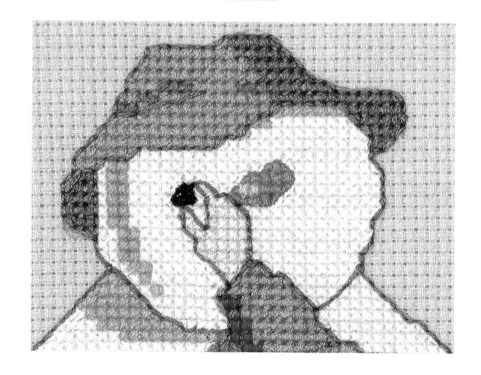

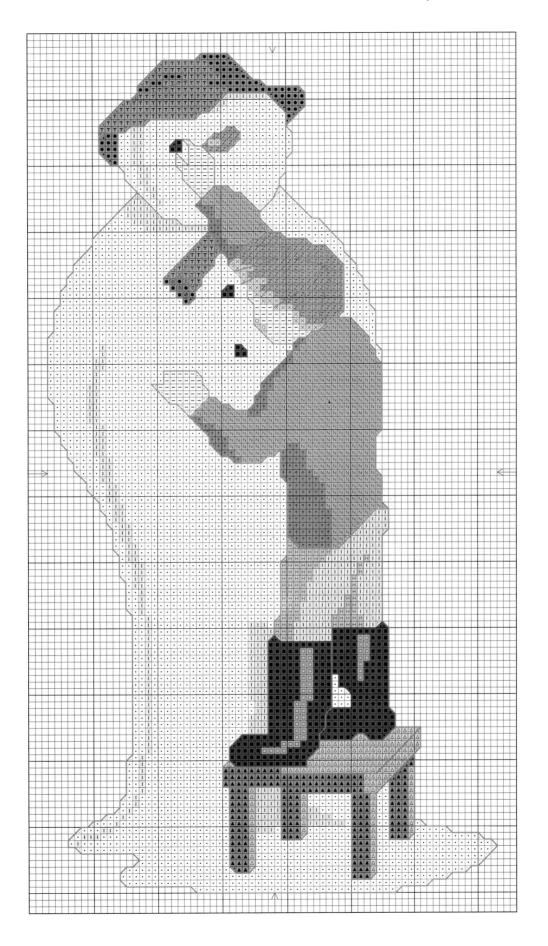

Snowman Cushion

When James stared out into the moonlit garden he could hardly believe his eyes – The Snowman moved! This cheerful cushion captures the moment when the magic begins.

You will need

- 14 count Aida in light blue, 35 x 35cm (14 x 14in)
- Stranded embroidery thread as given in the key
- No. 24 tapestry needle
- Approx. 1 metre (40in) blue fabric
- Cushion pad 46 x 46cm (18 x 18in)

FINISHED DESIGN SIZE
21 x 20.5cm (8¼ x 8in)

STITCHING THE DESIGN

1 Find the centre of your fabric by folding it in half from top to bottom, then again from left to right, and mark the centre with a pin or thread. Prepare the fabric following the instructions on page 104. Bind the edges with masking tape to prevent them fraying as you work.

2 Find the centre of the chart and mark it for your reference. Work with two strands of embroidery thread in your needle for the stitching and begin working on your design

from this central point. Each cross stitch is worked over a single square of the fabric and, for a neat effect, it is important to ensure that all the top stitches run in the same direction as each other.

3 Refer to the chart and key constantly to complete the cross stitching, remembering that each square of the chart represents one stitch. Use two strands of Grey 645 to back stitch the outline and Black 310 for The Snowman's mouth.

FINISHING THE CUSHION

4 When the stitching is complete, you can remove your finished embroidery from the frame or hoop and hand wash it gently in warm water. Then, lay the embroidery face down on a towel and gently press it with a warm iron until it is dry.

5 Cut a square of blue cotton of 43 x 43cm (17 x 17in) for the back of the cushion and set aside. From the remaining cotton, cut four strips of 10 x 48cm (4 x 19in). Trim the finished work to 30 x 30cm (12 x 12in).

6 With the right sides together, pin one of the strips to the top of the embroidery, leaving a seam allowance of 2cm (1/2in) along the edge of the design. Ensure that it is centrally placed and then sew it into place. Do not sew right to the edges; stop 2cm (1/2in) from the side edges of the embroidery to allow for the mitred corners. Sew on the bottom strip and then the two side strips, following the same method.

7 Mitre the corners, following the instructions given on page 107.

8 Press your work. With right sides together, sew the backing fabric to the front round three sides. Turn your cushion cover right side out, insert the cushion pad and hand stitch the fourth side closed.

SNOWMAN CUSHION		DMC	Anchor
·	White	blanc	2
■	Black	310	403
△	Beige	612	832
Z	Orange	721	324
X	Dark yellow	725	305
+	Pale blue	775	128
I	Dark blue	809	130
▲	Brown	869	944
▽	Pale yellow	3078	292
◻	Grey	645	273

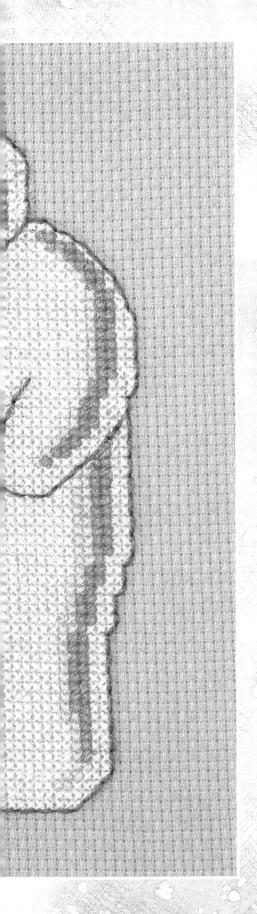

The Christmas Tree

The Snowman liked the Christmas tree – he
could see his face in the glittery decorations.

You *will* need

- 14 count Aida in light blue,
  35 x 33cm (14 x 13in)
- Stranded embroidery thread
  as given in the key
- No. 24 tapestry needle
- Strong card
- Strong thread for lacing
- Mount and frame of
  your choice

FINISHED DESIGN SIZE
15.5 x 13cm (6¼ x 5in)

STITCHING THE PANEL

1 Cut out the fabric, calculating the
amount you would like to remain
visible between the stitched design
and the frame and leaving enough to use
an embroidery frame. The amount
suggested will give approximately
5–7.5cm (2–3in) of unstitched fabric
all round the design.

2 Prepare the fabric as instructed on
page 104. Bind the edges with
masking tape to prevent them from
fraying. Fold your fabric in half
from top to bottom, then again from
left to right, and mark the centre
with a pin. You will start work here.

3 Find the centre of the chart and mark it for your reference. Work with two strands of embroidery thread in your needle and begin stitching your design from this central point. Each cross stitch is worked over a single square of Aida. For a tidy look, make sure all your top stitches run neatly in the same direction.

4 Refer to the chart and key constantly to complete the cross stitching, remembering that each square of the chart represents one stitch. Use two strands of Grey 645 for the back stitch details around the figures, as indicated on the chart. Use Brown 869 for the back stitch detail on the boy's face.

5 Stitch the Christmas tree baubles last. The tinsel threads have a tendency to divide as you use them. This does not detract from the finished work, but it tends to add to the glistening effect and creates an illusion of the fairy lights.

FINISHING THE PANEL

6 Take your finished embroidery out of the frame or hoop. It may look a little grubby, but in this case, you can hand wash it in warm water. To dry, lay it face down on a towel and press with a warm iron.

7 Choose a frame for the embroidery. Cut a piece of card to fit into the back of the frame and stretch the embroidery over it, following the instructions given on pages 106–7.

8 For the most dramatic effects, choose a mount in a colour that is not used much in the design. This could be the dark green or the orange, or perhaps you would like to pick a shade that complements your home décor. Assemble the glass (if desired), the mount and the embroidery in the frame and tape the backing board in place.

THE CHRISTMAS TREE			
	DMC	Anchor	Madeira no. 50
· White	blanc	2	
O Dark pink	224	893	
− Light pink	225	1026	
■ Black	310	403	
T Light green	470	267	
△ Beige	612	832	
Z Orange	721	324	
X Yellow	725	305	
+ Light blue	775	128	
I Dark blue	809	130	
▲ Brown	869	944	
● Dark green	937	268	
▽ Blue tinsel			402
✳ Gold tinsel			403
H Red tinsel			404
╲ Grey	645	273	

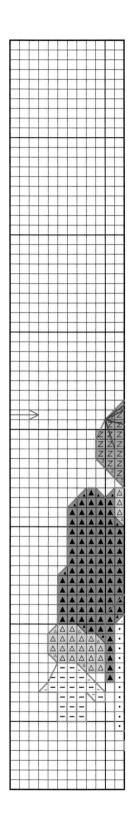

Festive Table Decorations

Decorate your festive table with these colourful and attractive designs to bring some Christmas spirit to your party.

You *will* need

- Stranded embroidery thread as given in the key
- No. 24 tapestry needle

For the cake frill:
- 5cm (2in) Aida band in white

FINISHED DESIGN SIZE
4.5cm (1³/4in) depth

For each napkin ring:
- Hardanger 22 count in white, 10 x 10cm (4 x 4in)
- Interfacing and napkin rings

FINISHED DESIGN SIZE
4.5 x 4cm (1³/4 x 1¹/2in)

STITCHING THE CAKE FRILL

1 Cut the Aida band to a length to suit your cake. Bind the ends with masking tape to prevent them from fraying as you work.

2 Begin stitching 1cm (¹/2in) in from the end and work your way along the length of the fabric, using two strands of embroidery thread in your needle. It is better to stitch this in your hand rather than using a frame. Work each cross stitch across one square of the fabric, making sure that all of the upper threads follow the same direction for a neat effect.

3 Refer to the chart and key constantly to complete the cross stitching, remembering that each square of the chart represents one stitch. Repeat the design to achieve the desired length.

FINISHING THE CAKE FRILL

4 When the stitching is complete, wash your finished embroidery carefully in warm water. Then, lay the embroidery face down on a towel and press it gently with a warm iron until it is dry.

5 Turn a small hem under at each end of the band and pin it around your cake.

STITCHING THE NAPKIN RINGS

1 Cut out the fabric to the size given on page 25. It is advisable to hold this design in your hand as you stitch, rather than using a hoop or ring. Find the centre point of your fabric square by folding it once top to bottom, then again left to right. Mark this starting point with a pin or thread.

2 Working with one strand of embroidery thread in your needle, start from the centre of the chart and begin stitching your design. Work each cross stitch over one pair of fabric threads, ensuring that the top stitches go in the same direction. Use Black 310 to back stitch the robin's legs and the Christmas bauble hanger.

FINISHING THE NAPKIN RINGS

3 When the stitching is complete, wash and dry your embroidery as described above for the cake frill (step 4).

4 Iron a square of interfacing onto the back of the design to cover the stitching and stiffen the design. Trim as close as possible to the stitched border and insert the fabric into your napkin ring. The interfacing should prevent the fabric wrinkling.

CAKE FRILL

		DMC	Anchor
Z	Red	321	9046
X	Yellow	725	305
+	Light blue	775	128
I	Dark blue	809	130

ROBIN NAPKIN RING

		DMC	Anchor
■	Black	310	403
△	Beige	612	832
X	Yellow	725	305
I	Blue	809	130
▲	Brown	869	944

BAUBLE NAPKIN RING

		DMC	Anchor
•	Cream	ecru	387
Z	Red	309	42
■	Black	310	403
O	Pink	760	1022
I	Blue	809	130

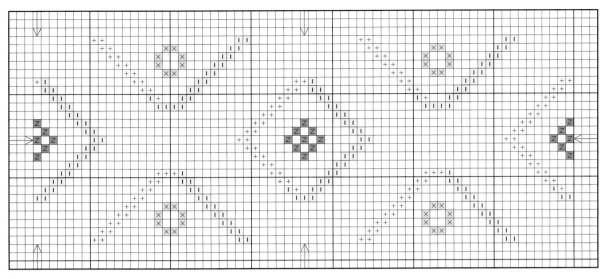

Cake frill

Robin napkin ring

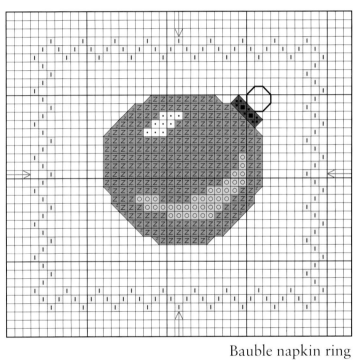

Bauble napkin ring

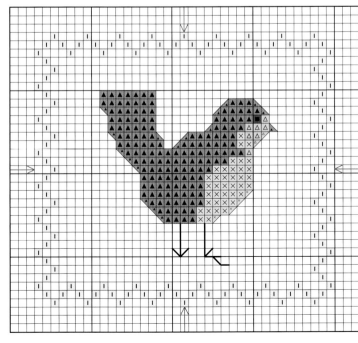

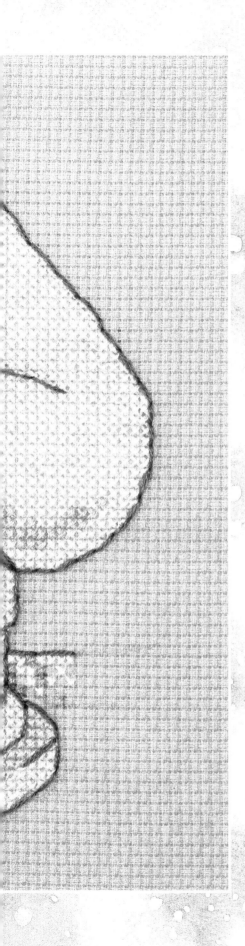

The Christmas Cake

The Snowman was thrilled to find another

snowman on the Christmas cake in James's house.

The little model looked just like him.

You will need

- 14 count Aida in light blue,
  35 x 33cm (14 x 13in)
- Stranded embroidery
  thread as given in the key
- No. 24 tapestry needle
- Strong card
- Strong thread for lacing
- Mount and frame of
  your choice

FINISHED DESIGN SIZE
15 x 12.5cm (6 x 5in)

STITCHING THE PANEL

1 Cut out the fabric, bearing in mind the amount you would like to remain visible between the stitched design and the frame and leaving enough to use an embroidery frame. The amount suggested will give roughly 5–7.5cm (2–3in) of unstitched fabric all round your design.

2 Prepare the fabric as instructed on page 104. Bind the edges with masking tape to prevent them from

fraying. Fold your fabric in half from top to bottom, then again from left to right, and mark the centre point of the fabric with a pin or thread. You will start stitching here.

3 Find the centre of the chart and mark it for your reference. Work with two strands of embroidery thread in your needle throughout and begin stitching your design from this central point. Work each cross stitch across one square of the fabric. Make sure that all your top stitches are in the same direction to give a neat finished effect.

4 Refer to the chart and key constantly to complete the cross stitching, remembering that each square of the chart represents one stitch. Use two strands of Black 310 to back stitch The Snowman's mouth and Grey 645 to outline the figures.

5 Use a single strand of Red 309 for the decorations round the side of the cake.

FINISHING THE PANEL

6 Take your finished embroidery out of the frame or hoop you have been working in. If it is looking grubby, you can hand wash it carefully in warm water. To dry, lay it face down on a towel and press it gently with a warm iron.

7 Choose a frame for the embroidery. Cut a piece of card to fit into the back of the frame and stretch the embroidery over it as explained on pages 106–7.

8 It is more effective to co-ordinate your mount with one of the lesser-used colours in the design. For a dramatic effect, why not pick out the bright red of the cake decorations? Assemble the glass (if desired), the mount and the embroidery in the frame and tape the backing board in place.

THE CHRISTMAS CAKE		DMC	Anchor
·	White	blanc	2
S	Cream	ecru	387
−	Dark pink	225	1026
■	Black	310	403
△	Beige	612	832
Z	Orange	721	324
X	Yellow	725	305
+	Pale blue	775	128
I	Dark blue	809	130
▲	Brown	869	944
●	Green	937	268
N	Turquoise	3809	169
▣	Silver	ART281	KBF
⟍	Grey	645	273
⟍	Red	309	42

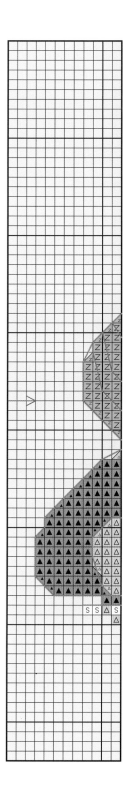

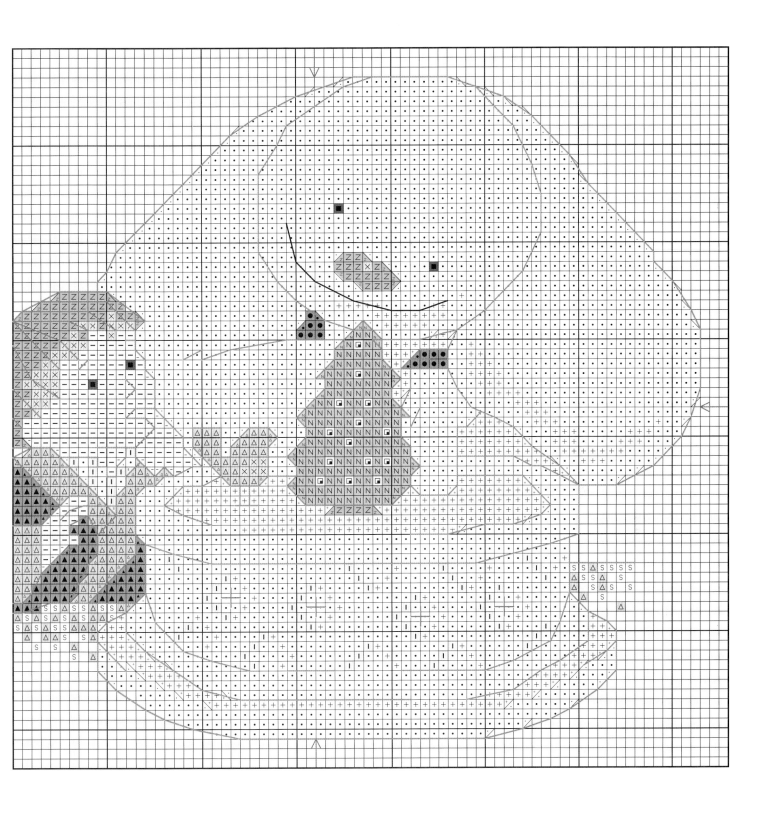

Baby Layette

Balloons in bright primary colours make a pretty decoration for your baby's bootees, bib, vest and towel, or you could adapt the designs for other accessories and items of clothing.

You will need

- Stranded embroidery thread as given in the keys
- No. 24 tapestry needle
- No. 28 sharp needle

For the bootees:

- Baby bootees (see Suppliers, page 108)

FINISHED DESIGN SIZE

2.5 x 3cm (1 x 1¹/4in)

For the bib:

- Bib (see Suppliers, page 108)

FINISHED DESIGN SIZE

10 x 5cm (4 x 2in)

For the vest:

- Baby vest of your choice
- Piece of waste canvas 7cm (3in) square

FINISHED DESIGN SIZE

2.5 x 5cm (1 x 2in)

For the towel:

- Guest towel 50 x 30cm (19 x 12in) (see Suppliers, page 108)

FINISHED DESIGN SIZE

40 x 22cm (16 x 8³/4in)

STITCHING THE BOOTEES

1 The area for stitching on the front of the bootees is so small that it is immediately apparent where the design has to go. Work with two strands of embroidery thread in your needle for all the stitching and begin working from the central point of the chart.

2 Work each cross stitch across one square of the fabric, ensuring that the upper strands of each stitch follow the same direction to give a neat effect.

3 Refer to the chart and key constantly to complete the cross stitching, remembering that each square of the chart represents one stitch. Use two strands of Black 310 to back stitch the balloon strings.

FINISHING THE BOOTEES

4 When the stitching is complete, hand wash the bootees carefully in warm water. Pat them with a clean towel then leave to dry naturally.

STITCHING THE BIB

1 Find the centre of the bib by folding it in half from top to bottom and then from left to right. Mark the centre point for reference with a pin or thread.

2 Begin stitching the purple balloon in the centre of the chart. Use two threads in your needle and complete the design by following the chart. Use Black 310 for the balloon strings, which are in back stitch.

FINISHING THE BIB

3 Hand wash the bib carefully in warm water. Lay it face down on a towel and press gently with a hot iron until it is dry.

STITCHING THE VEST

1 Tack the piece of waste fabric onto the vest in the position you require the design to be. It helps to mark with a pin where you want the centre of the design to lie.

2 Work the cross stitches in the usual way using two strands of embroidery thread. It helps to use a sharper needle on this fabric (no. 28 is recommended) but it is not imperative. It is really important, however, to make sure that the points of all the cross stitches touch each other neatly.

3 Refer to the chart for the colours required on each square. Use Black 310 for the balloon strings.

FINISHING THE VEST

4 When the stitching is complete, take out the tacking stitches and trim the waste canvas to about 2.5cm (1in) around the embroidery. Using a small sponge or tissue, moisten the waste canvas threads all over until they become limp.

5 Using a pair of tweezers, gently pull out the waste canvas threads one by one so as not to distort the stitching. They should

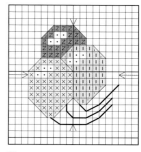

Bootees

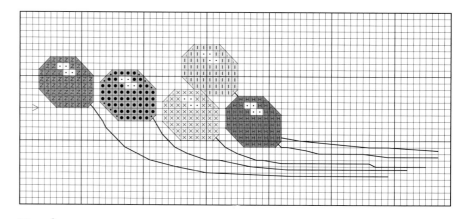

Towel

come out quite easily. It is easier to remove the threads that run in one direction first and then in the other direction.

6 Wash your work thoroughly when you have finished to remove any starch that may have come from the waste canvas.

STITCHING THE TOWEL

1 Fold the band on the towel in half lengthways then from left to right to find the centre. Mark it with a pin or thread.

2 Begin stitching the purple balloon 29 squares left of the centre of the chart. Use two threads throughout for the cross stitch and two threads for the back stitch.

3 Follow the chart for the colours required on each square and where to use back stitch. Use two strands of Black 310 to back stitch the balloon strings.

FINISHING THE TOWEL

4 When the stitching is complete, hand wash the towel carefully in warm water. Lay it face down on a towel and press gently with a hot iron until it is completely dry and ready for use.

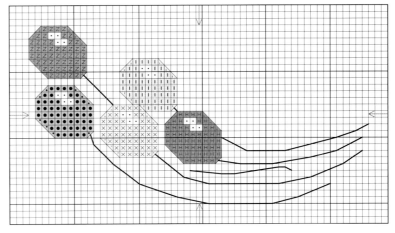

Bib

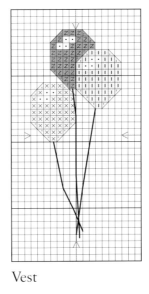

Vest

BOOTEES AND VEST

		DMC	Anchor
·	White	blanc	2
Z	Red	606	335
I	Blue	809	130
×	Yellow	973	297
◿	Black	310	403

BIB AND TOWEL

		DMC	Anchor
·	White	blanc	2
Z	Red	606	335
●	Green	702	226
I	Blue	809	130
H	Purple	915	1029
×	Yellow	973	297
◿	Black	310	403

Towel

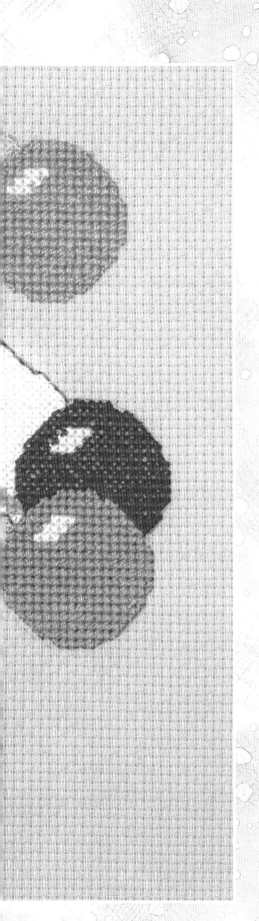

Cloud of Balloons

James and The Snowman fell over in a cloud of balloons. "Are you alright?" asked James and The Snowman nodded.

You will need

- 14 count Aida in light blue, 38 x 35cm (15 x 14in)
- Stranded embroidery thread as given in the key
- No. 24 tapestry needle
- Strong card
- Strong thread for lacing
- Mount and frame of your choice

FINISHED DESIGN SIZE
18.5 x 15.5cm (7¼ x 6in)

STITCHING THE PANEL

1 Cut out the fabric, bearing in mind the amount you would like to remain visible between the stitched design and the frame and leaving enough excess to use an embroidery frame. The amount suggested will result in approximately 5–7.5cm (2–3in) of unstitched fabric all round.

2 Prepare the fabric as instructed on page 104. Bind the edges with masking tape to prevent them from fraying. Find the centre of your fabric and mark it with a pin or thread.

3 Find the centre of the chart and mark it for your reference. Work with two strands of embroidery thread in your needle and begin stitching your design from this central point. Work each cross stitch across one square of the fabric, ensuring that the top stitches follow the same direction.

4 Refer to the chart and key constantly to complete the cross stitching, remembering that each square of the chart represents one stitch. Use two strands of Grey 645 to back stitch the outlines of the figures, as indicated on the chart.

5 Use two strands of Brown 869 for the back stitch detail on the boy's face, Black 310 for The Snowman's features and Dark blue 809 for the dressing gown cord.

FINISHING THE PANEL

6 When the stitching is complete, remove your finished embroidery from the frame or hoop and hand wash it carefully in warm water. To dry, lay the embroidery face down on a towel and press it with a warm iron.

7 Choose a frame for the embroidery. Cut a piece of card to fit into the back of the frame and stretch the embroidery over it, as explained on pages 106–7.

8 Your mount should be in a colour that complements the embroidery and co-ordinates with your décor. Choose a colour that only features slightly in the design – perhaps the dark blue or dark green. Assemble the glass (if desired), the mount and the embroidery in the frame and tape the backing board in place.

CLOUD OF BALLOONS		DMC	Anchor
·	White	blanc	2
◎	Dark pink	224	893
—	Light pink	225	1026
■	Black	310	403
▽	Red	355	1014
T	Light green	470	267
△	Beige	612	832
▢	Grey	645	273
Z	Orange	721	324
✕	Yellow	725	305
+	Light blue	775	128
I	Dark blue	809	130
▲	Brown	869	944
●	Dark green	937	268

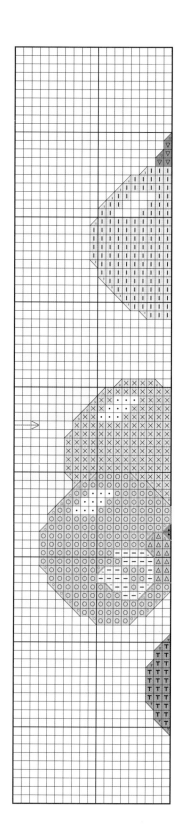

Riding the Motorbike

The Snowman started the engine and turned on
the headlamp. James was clinging onto The Snowman as
the motorbike roared away into the night sky.

You will need

- 14 count Aida in navy blue,
  36 x 38cm (14 x 15in)
- Stranded embroidery thread as given in the key
- No. 24 tapestry needle
- Strong card
- Strong thread for lacing
- Mount and frame of your choice

FINISHED DESIGN SIZE

13 x 17cm (5³/4 x 6³/4in)

STITCHING THE PANEL

1 Cut out the fabric, deciding the amount you
would like to remain visible between the stitched
design and the frame. The measurements suggested
will leave 5–7.5cm (2–3in) of unstitched fabric.

2 Prepare the fabric as instructed on page 104.
Bind the edges with masking tape to prevent
them from fraying. Fold the fabric in half from top
to bottom, then again from left to right, and mark
the centre point with a pin or thread.

3 Find the centre of the chart and mark it for your reference. Work with two strands of embroidery thread in your needle and begin stitching your design from this central point. Work each cross stitch across one square of the fabric, ensuring that the top stitch of each cross stitch follows the same direction for a neat effect.

4 Refer to the chart and key constantly to complete the cross stitching, remembering that each square of the chart represents one stitch. Use two strands of Light red 3350 for the back stitch details on the scarf and the headlamp, as indicated on the chart. For all other back stitch, use two strands of Black 310.

5 Finish by using silver thread for the stars. You may find that it splits in use, but this will just add to the glittery effect.

FINISHING THE PANEL

6 Remove your finished embroidery from the frame or hoop. If it looks grubby, hand wash it in warm water. Lay it face down on a towel and press it gently with a warm iron until it is dry.

7 Choose a frame for the embroidery. Cut a piece of card to fit into the back of the frame and stretch the embroidery over it as explained on pages 106–7.

8 Pick out a colour for your frame or mount that only features slightly in the design – perhaps the dark red of The Snowman's crash helmet. Assemble the glass (if desired), the mount and the embroidery in the frame and tape the backing board in place.

RIDING THE MOTORBIKE		DMC	Anchor
·	White	blanc	2
▣	Dark yellow	307	289
■	Black	310	403
↑	Medium pink grey	452	232
H	Light pink grey	453	231
U	Light yellow	727	293
N	Blue	932	1033
S	Light purple	3042	870
▽	Light red	3350	65
✳	Dark red	3685	1028
L	Dark purple	3740	873
F	Rust	3830	5975
☐	Silver	ART281	KBF

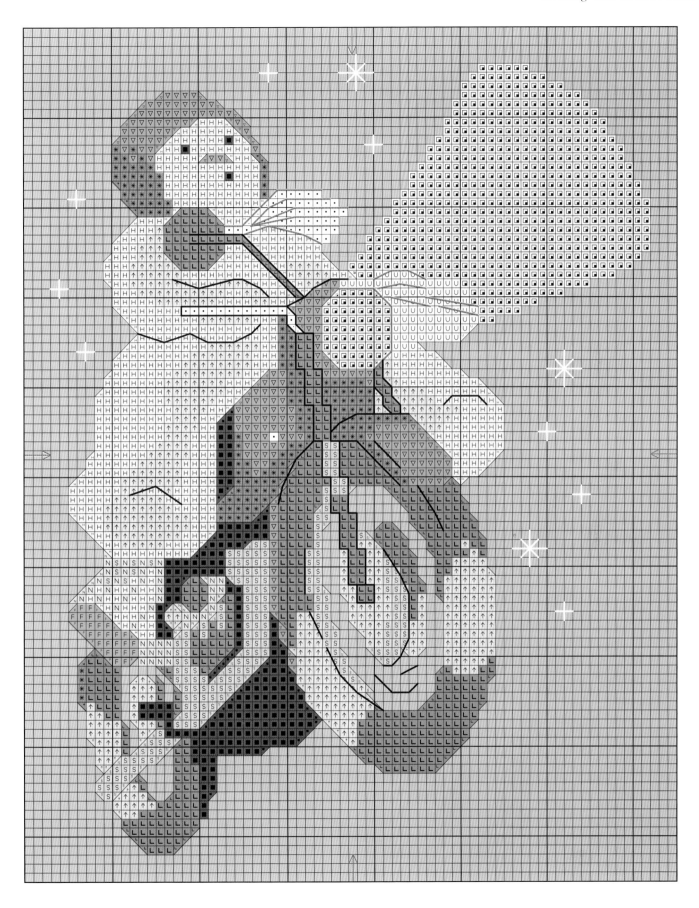

Animal Accessories

These enchanting wildlife designs could be applied to all sorts of accessories, to make original gifts that anyone would be delighted to receive.

You *will need*
- Stranded embroidery thread as given in the keys
- No. 24 tapestry needle

For the bookmark:
- 14 count Aida in Rustico, 20 x 25cm (8in x 10in)

FINISHED SIZE
6 x 15cm (2¹/₂ x 6in)

For the key ring:
- Evenweave 22 count fabric 10 x 10cm (4 x 4in)
- Key ring

FINISHED SIZE
4.5 x 4.5cm (1³/₄ x 1³/₄in)

STITCHING THE BOOKMARK

1 Begin your stitching at the bottom of the design, using two strands of embroidery thread in your needle. It is easier to hold the fabric in your hand rather than in a frame or hoop.

2 Follow the chart, making one cross stitch for each square and checking against the key to work out the correct colours for each. Use two strands of Black 310 to back stitch the branches of the trees and Brown 869 for the back stitch details on the owl.

FINISHING THE BOOKMARK

3 When the stitching is complete, hand wash your embroidery carefully in warm water. Then, lay the embroidery face down on a towel and press it gently with a warm iron until it is completely dry.

4 Trim the fabric to 2.5cm (1in) from the top and bottom. Fray the fabric down to the stitched brown border. Measure 5cm (2in) in from the side borders and trim.

5 Fold the fabric under, leaving 3mm (1/8in) at each side of the design and press. Place one flap over the other at the back and turn under the narrow seam allowance neatly along the edge of the bookmark. Slip stitch along the length of the bookmark and press it once again with a warm iron.

STITCHING THE KEY RING

1 Hold the fabric in your hand to work on it. Use one strand of embroidery thread throughout this project and make your stitches across two strands.

2 Begin in the centre of the chart, making one cross stitch over two threads of the fabric and following the colours marked. Use Grey 645 for the outline of the rabbit.

FINISHING THE KEY RING

3 When the stitching is complete, hand wash your embroidery in warm water. To dry, lay it face down on a towel and press it gently with a warm iron. Insert your embroidery into the key ring.

RABBIT KEY RING		
	DMC	Anchor
■ Black	310	403
☒ Yellow	3078	292
▲ Brown	869	944
◩ Grey	645	273

OWL BOOKMARK

	DMC	Anchor
− Cream	ecru	387
■ Black	310	403
Z Brown	801	359
▲ Dark beige	841	378
△ Beige	842	376

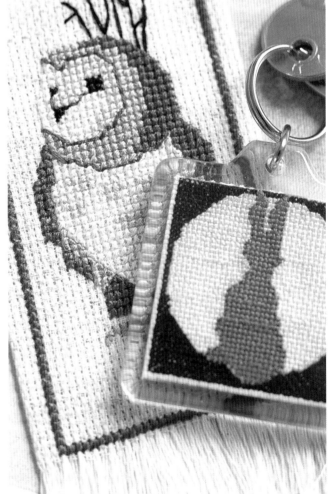

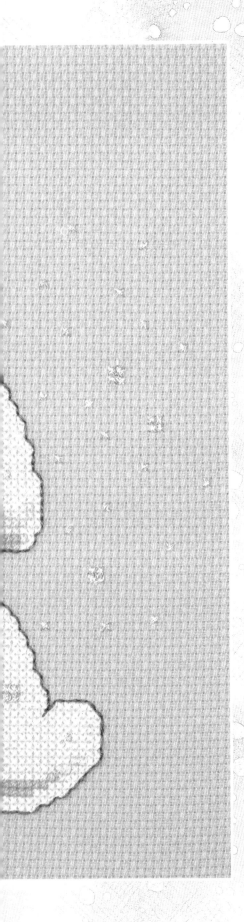

Running

The Snowman gripped James's hand and began to run across the garden, bounding, jumping, leaping, until James found they were flying!

You will need

- 14 count Aida in light blue, 41 x 38cm (16 x 15in)
- Stranded embroidery thread as given in the key
- No. 24 tapestry needle
- Strong card
- Strong thread for lacing
- Mount and frame of your choice

FINISHED DESIGN SIZE
23.5 x 18cm (9¼ x 7¼in)

STITCHING THE PANEL

1 Cut out the fabric, after deciding the amount you would like to remain visible between the stitched design and the frame. The amount suggested will give approximately 5–7.5cm (2–3in) of unstitched fabric all round the design.

2 Prepare the fabric as instructed on page 104. Bind the edges with masking tape to prevent them from fraying. Find the centre of your fabric by folding it in half from top to bottom, then again from left to right. Mark the centre with a pin or thread.

3 Find the centre of the chart and mark it for your reference. Work with two strands of embroidery thread

in your needle and begin stitching your design from this central point. Work each cross stitch across one square of the fabric. Make sure that the top part of each stitch runs in the same direction. The neater your stitches, the more professional the finished design will look.

4 Refer to the chart and key constantly to complete the cross stitching, remembering that each square of the chart represents one stitch. Use two strands of Grey 645 for most of the back stitch details, as indicated on the chart. Use Brown 869 for the back stitch detail on the boy's face.

5 Use the metallic thread last to stitch the stars. This thread has a tendency to split in use but don't worry – it will enhance the glittery effect.

FINISHING THE PANEL

6 When the stitching is complete, remove your finished embroidery from the frame or hoop and hand wash it in warm water. To dry, lay the embroidery face down on a towel and press it with a warm iron.

7 Choose a frame for your embroidery. Cut a piece of card to fit into the back of the frame and stretch the embroidery over it following the instructions on pages 106–7.

8 When selecting the colour of your mount, you can choose one that complements the décor in your home, or you can pick out a colour in the design. It is most effective to choose colours that only feature slightly in the design. Assemble the glass (if desired), the mount and the embroidery in the frame and tape the backing board in place.

RUNNING		
	DMC	Anchor
· White	blanc	2
O Dark pink	224	893
− Light pink	225	1026
■ Black	310	403
T Light green	470	267
△ Beige	612	832
□ Grey	645	273
Z Orange	721	324
X Yellow	725	305
+ Light blue	775	128
I Dark blue	809	130
▲ Brown	869	944
● Dark green	937	268
▣ Silver	ART 281	KBF

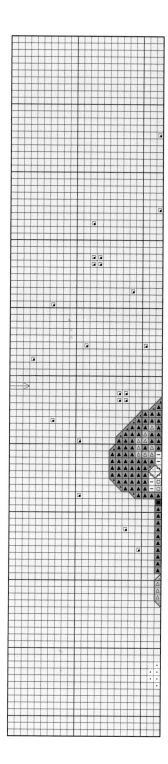

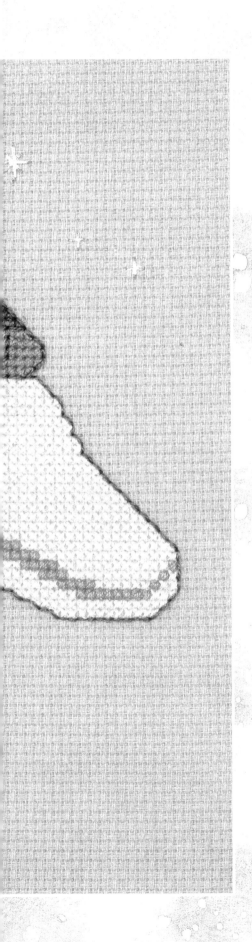

Walking in the Air

This is the famous scene from The Snowman story where James and The Snowman fly to the North Pole. It is hard to stitch this design without humming the music at the same time!

You *will* need

- 14 count Aida in light blue, 38 x 33cm (15 x 13in)
- Stranded embroidery thread as given in the key
- No. 24 tapestry needle
- Strong card
- Strong thread for lacing
- Mount and frame of your choice

FINISHED DESIGN SIZE
17 x 13cm (6³/4 x 5¹/4in)

STITCHING THE PANEL

1 Cut out the fabric, after deciding the amount you would like to remain visible between the stitched design and the frame. The measurements suggested will result in approximately 5–7.5cm (2–3in) of unstitched fabric all round.

2 Prepare the fabric as instructed on page 104. Bind the edges with masking tape to prevent them from fraying. Find the centre of your fabric by folding it in half from top to bottom, then again from left to right, and mark the centre with a pin or thread.

3 Next, find the centre of the chart and
mark it for your reference. Work with
two strands of embroidery thread in your
needle and begin stitching your design from
this central point. Work each cross stitch
across one square of the fabric. Always make
sure that the top stitches follow the same
direction with their points touching.

4 Refer to the chart and key constantly
to complete the cross stitching,
remembering that each square of the chart
represents one stitch. Use two strands of
Grey 645 for most of the back stitch details,
as indicated on the chart. Use Brown 869 to
back stitch the boy's mouth and hair.

5 Use silver thread to stitch the stars. This
thread has a tendency to split in use but
this will just enhance the glittery effect.

FINISHING THE PANEL

6 Remove your finished embroidery from
the frame or hoop and, if it is grubby,
hand wash it carefully in warm water.
Lay the wet embroidery face down on
a towel and press it gently with a warm
iron until it is completely dry.

7 Choose a frame for the embroidery. Cut
a piece of card to fit into the back of the
frame and stretch the embroidery over it as
explained on pages 106–7.

8 Choose a mount for the embroidery that
will co-ordinate with the colours in the
design and with your home furnishings. Pick
out a colour that only features slightly in the
design – perhaps the blue stripe of the boy's
pyjamas – for a stunning finished effect.
Assemble the glass (if desired), the mount
and the embroidery in the frame and tape
the backing board in place.

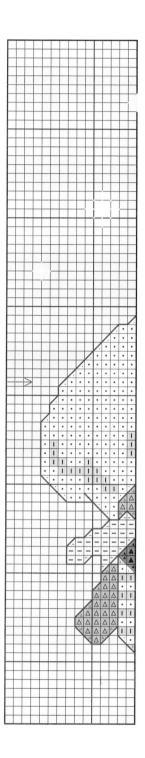

WALKING IN THE AIR		
	DMC	Anchor
· White	blanc	2
O Dark pink	224	893
− Light pink	225	1026
▓ Black	310	403
T Light green	470	267
△ Beige	612	832
▢ Grey	645	273
Z Orange	721	324
✕ Yellow	725	305
I Dark blue	809	130
▲ Brown	869	944
◉ Dark green	937	268
▢ Silver	ART 281	KBF

Christmas Tree Settings

This simple Christmas tree design looks stunning on Christmas napkins and tablemats.

You will need

- Stranded embroidery thread as given in the key
- No. 24 tapestry needle

For the tablemat:

- Evenweave 30 count linen in pale blue, 30.5 x 47cm (12 x 18½in)

FINISHED DESIGN SIZE
56 x 42cm (22 x 16½in)

For the napkins:

- Evenweave 30 count linen in pale blue 35.5 x 35.5cm (14 x 14in) for each napkin

FINISHED DESIGN SIZE
29 x 29cm (11½ x 11½in)

STITCHING THE TABLEMAT

1 Fold the fabric in half lengthways, measure 10cm (4in) in from one of the short edges and pin or mark with a thread. Begin your stitching at this point, referring to the arrow on the base of the chart which indicates the starting point.

2 Use two strands of embroidery thread in your needle and make each stitch over two threads of linen, ensuring that all your top stitches point in the same direction. Remember that each square on the chart represents one stitch and follow the colours.

FINISHING THE TABLEMAT

3 When the stitching is complete, hand wash your tablemat carefully in warm water. Then, lay the embroidery face down on a towel and press it gently with a warm iron until it is completely dry.

4 Hem the edges using a matching blue thread (see page 107). Turn under the hem edges twice and stitch each hem by hand. A neater effect is achieved if you mitre the corners. To do this, press a single hem to the wrong side. Then open the hem out again and fold the corner of the fabric inwards. Refold the hem to the wrong side along the pressed line and slip stitch into place.

STITCHING THE NAPKINS

1 Measure 5cm (2in) diagonally in from the corner of the napkin and begin stitching the base of the Christmas tree motif. Use two strands of embroidery thread throughout.

2 Follow the chart for the colours to be used on each square, and make sure your top threads run in the same direction for a neat finished effect.

FINISHING THE NAPKINS

3 Hand wash your napkins in warm water and press them in a towel to dry.

4 To hem your napkins, follow the instructions given for the tablemat (step 4), and see also page 107.

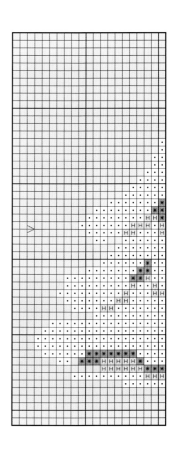

TABLEMAT AND NAPKINS		
	DMC	Anchor
· White	blanc	2
✳ Dark green	699	923
H Light green	3819	278

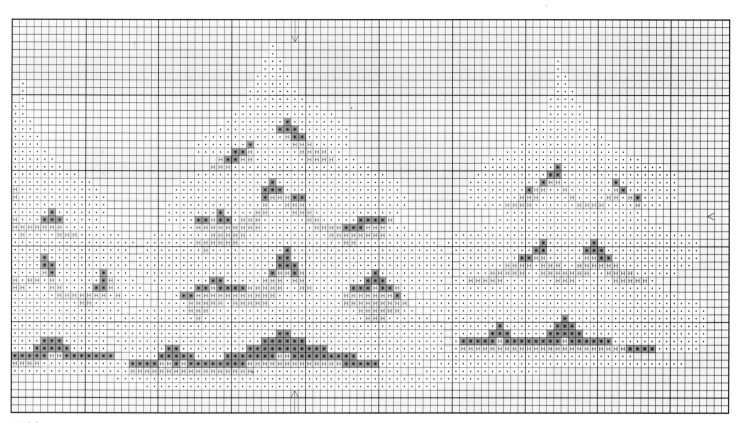

Tablemat

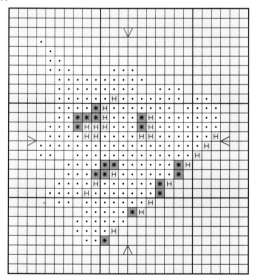

Napkin

The Icy Wilderness

James and The Snowman landed in the icy
North after an exciting journey through the sky. All around
them was a great forest of pine trees laden with snow.

You will need

- 14 count Aida in light blue,
  36 x 38cm (14 x 15in)
- Stranded embroidery thread
  as given in the key
- No. 24 tapestry needle
- Strong card
- Strong thread for lacing
- Mount and frame of your choice

FINISHED DESIGN SIZE
14.5 x 18.5cm (5³/4 x 7¹/4in)

STITCHING THE PANEL

1 Cut out the fabric, leaving enough excess
to form a border around the design and
use an embroidery frame. The measurements
suggested will give approximately 5–7.5cm
(2–3in) of unstitched fabric all round.

2 Prepare the fabric as instructed on page
104. Bind the edges with masking tape to
prevent them from fraying. Fold your fabric in
half from top to bottom, then again from left
to right, to find the centre point, then mark
this with a pin or thread.

3 Find the centre of the chart and mark it for your reference. Work with two strands of embroidery thread in your needle and begin stitching your design from this central point. Work each cross stitch across one square of the fabric. For a neat final effect, make sure that the top stitches run in the same direction.

4 Refer to the chart and key constantly to complete the cross stitching, remembering that each square of the chart represents one stitch. Use two strands of Grey 645 for most of the back stitch details, as indicated on the chart. Use Black 310 to back stitch The Snowman's mouth.

FINISHING THE PANEL

5 When the stitching is complete, remove your finished embroidery from the frame or hoop. If it needs it, hand wash your design carefully in warm water. Then, lay the embroidery face down on a towel and press it gently with a warm iron to dry it.

6 Choose a frame for the embroidery. Cut a piece of card to fit into the back of the frame and stretch the embroidery over it as explained on pages 106–7.

7 The colour of your mount should co-ordinate with the colours in the embroidery and with your home décor. Pick out a colour that only features slightly in the design – perhaps the orange of the boy's hair or the black of the buttons. Assemble the glass (if desired), the mount and the embroidery in the frame and tape the backing board in place.

THE ICY WILDERNESS		DMC	Anchor
·	White	blanc	2
O	Dark pink	224	893
−	Pale pink	225	1026
■	Black	310	403
T	Light green	470	267
△	Beige	612	832
Z	Orange	721	324
×	Yellow	725	305
+	Light blue	775	128
I	Dark blue	809	130
▲	Brown	869	944
●	Dark green	937	268
◺	Grey	645	273

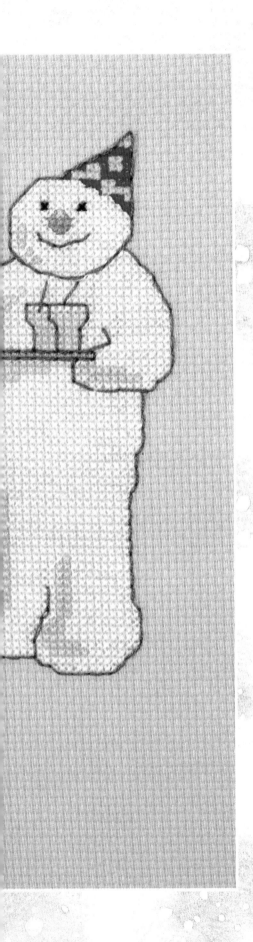

Joining the Party

James and The Snowman could hear music ahead. When they arrived at the North Pole, they were invited to join a snowmen's party. The snowmen began to dance – with James in the middle.

You will need

- 14 count Aida in light blue, 41 x 38cm (16 x 15in)
- Stranded embroidery thread as given in the key
- No. 24 tapestry needle
- Strong card
- Strong thread for lacing
- Mount and frame of your choice

FINISHED DESIGN SIZE
20 x 17.5cm (7³/4 x 7in)

STITCHING THE PANEL

1 Cut out the fabric, calculating the amount you would like to remain visible between the stitched design and the frame and leaving enough to use an embroidery frame. The amount suggested will give approximately 5–7.5cm (2–3in) of unstitched fabric round the design.

2 Prepare the fabric as instructed on page 104. Bind the edges with masking tape to prevent them from fraying. Find the centre point of your fabric and mark it with a pin or thread.

3 Find the centre of the chart and mark it for your reference. Work with two strands of embroidery thread in your needle and begin stitching your design from this central point. Each cross stitch is worked over one square of fabric. For a tidy finished effect, make sure all your top stitches run neatly in the same direction.

4 Refer to the chart and key constantly to complete the cross stitching, remembering that each square of the chart represents one stitch. Use two strands of Grey 645 to back stitch the outline and for the snowmen's mouths and arms.

FINISHING THE PANEL

5 Take your finished embroidery out of the frame or hoop. It may look a little grubby, in which case you can hand wash it in warm water. To dry, lay it face down on a towel and press with a warm iron.

6 Choose a frame for the embroidery. Cut a piece of card to fit into the back of the frame and stretch the embroidery over it following the instructions on pages 106–7.

7 For the most dramatic effects, choose a mount in a colour that is not used much in the design. This could be the yellow or brown, or perhaps you would like to pick another shade that complements your home furnishings. Assemble the glass (if desired), the mount and the embroidery in the frame and tape the backing board in place.

JOINING THE PARTY		DMC	Anchor
·	White	blanc	2
O	Dark pink	224	893
–	Light pink	225	1026
■	Black	310	403
H	Red	321	9046
T	Light green	470	267
△	Beige	612	832
Z	Orange	721	324
X	Yellow	725	305
+	Pale blue	775	128
I	Dark blue	809	130
▲	Brown	869	944
●	Dark green	937	268
◺	Grey	645	273

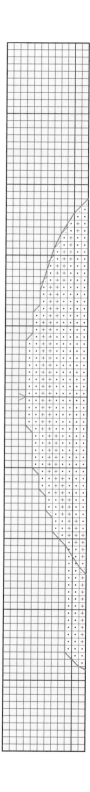

The Scottish Dancer

James danced with snowmen from all over the world.
The Scottish snowman wore a traditional kilt. This panel uses
different coloured threads from most of the others, to
embroider the brightly coloured tartan.

You will need

- 14 count Aida in light blue,
  35 x 38cm (14 x 15in)
- Stranded embroidery thread
  as given in the key
- No. 24 tapestry needle
- Strong card
- Strong thread for lacing
- Mount and frame of your choice

FINISHED DESIGN SIZE
15 x 18.5cm (6 x 7¼in)

STITCHING THE PANEL

1 Cut out the fabric, bearing in mind the amount you would like to remain visible between the stitched design and the frame. The measurements suggested will result in approximately 5–7.5cm (2–3in) of unstitched fabric all round the design.

2 Prepare the fabric as instructed on page 104. Bind the edges with masking tape to prevent them from fraying. Find the centre of your fabric by folding it in half from top to bottom, then again from left to right, and mark the centre with a pin or thread. You will start working here.

3 Find the centre of the chart and mark it for your reference. Work with two strands of embroidery thread in your needle and begin stitching your design from this central point. Work each cross stitch across one square of the fabric, ensuring that the top stitches follow the same direction. Keep your stitches neat.

4 Refer to the chart and key constantly to complete the cross stitching, remembering that each square of the chart represents one stitch.

5 Use two strands of Russet 919 for the back stitch on the kilt, Grey 645 for the outline and Black 310 for the mouth.

FINISHING THE PANEL

6 When the stitching is complete, you can remove your finished embroidery from the frame or hoop and hand wash it carefully in warm water. To dry, lay it face down on a towel and press it with a warm iron.

7 Choose a frame for your embroidery. Cut a piece of card to fit into the back of the frame and stretch the embroidery over it as explained on pages 106–7.

8 This brightly coloured design would look even more dramatic if you choose a mount in one of the stunning colours of the kilt – brown, russet or turquoise. This will highlight the colour you choose in the design. Assemble the glass (if desired), the mount and the embroidery in the frame and tape the backing board in place.

THE SCOTTISH DANCER

		DMC	Anchor
.	White	blanc	2
■	Black	310	403
H	Turquoise	597	168
△	Beige	612	832
Z	Orange	721	324
+	Pale blue	775	128
I	Dark blue	809	130
▲	Brown	869	944
*	Russet	919	340
◩	Grey	645	273

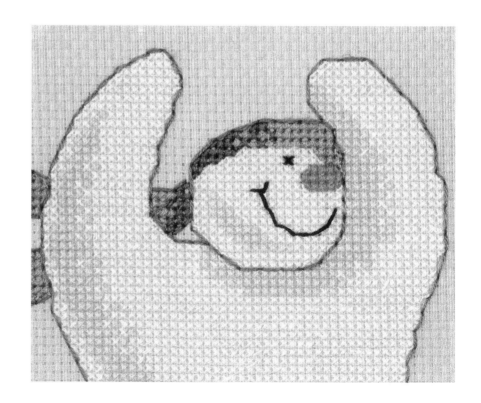

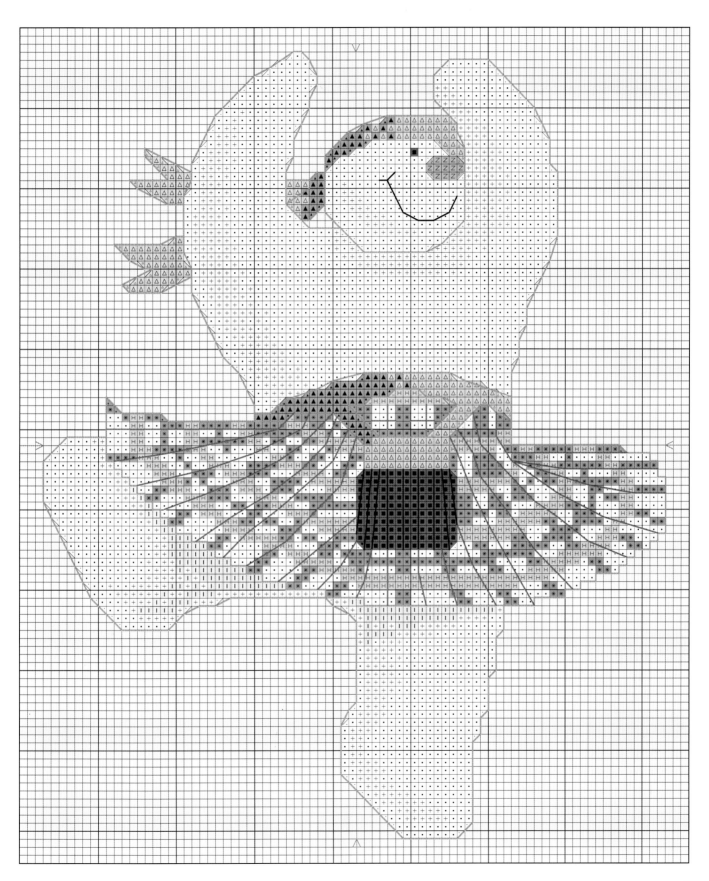

Dancing Snowmen

They whirled and twirled until they were giddy. James gave his Snowman a big hug. These designs for a mug and coaster would work equally well on cushion covers, napkins, tablemats or any other accessories you wish to decorate.

You will need
- Stranded embroidery thread as given in the key
- No. 24 tapestry needle

For the mug:
- Mug designed to take cross stitch (see Suppliers, page 108)
- 14 count Aida in light blue, 23.5 x 8cm (9^{1}/$_4$ x 3^{1}/$_4$in)

FINISHED DESIGN SIZE
23.5 x 8cm (9^{1}/$_4$ x 3^{1}/$_4$in)

For the coasters:
- Square coasters that will take a piece of cross stitch measuring 7.5 x 7cm (3 x 2^{3}/$_4$in) (see Suppliers, page 108)
- Evenweave 30 count fabric in white, 15 x 15cm (6 x 6in)

FINISHED DESIGN SIZE
7.5 x 7cm (3 x 2^{3}/$_4$in)

STITCHING THE MUG

1 When you buy a mug specially adapted for taking a cross stitch design, it will be supplied with a piece of fabric in place. This is usually the size given on page 73 but check before you cut out your own choice of fabric. The measurements on page 73 allow extra fabric for working in a frame.

2 Use two strands of embroidery thread in your needle and begin stitching at the point indicated on the left of the chart. Follow the colours indicated on the chart, referring to the key. Remember that each stitch is worked over two threads of fabric and corresponds to one square on the chart.

3 Use two strands of Grey 645 for the back stitch around the figures.

FINISHING THE MUG

4 When you have finished your embroidery, wash it gently in warm water then dry it by laying it face down on a towel and pressing it with a warm iron.

5 Trim the fabric to the template size. Insert your design into the mug and use a small sliver of sticky tape to hold it in position. Insert the centre portion of the mug and it is then ready for use.

STITCHING THE COASTER

1 Cut your piece of fabric for the first coaster to the size indicated on page 73. Fold it in half lengthways and then in half horizontally to find the centre and mark this point with a pin or thread.

2 Begin stitching at the centre, using two strands of embroidery thread throughout. Follow the colours on the chart. Each stitch should cross two threads of the fabric, and the top stitches should all point in the same direction.

3 Use two strands of Black 310 for the back stitch on the hat and on James's hair. Use Grey 645 for all other outlines.

FINISHING THE COASTER

4 When the embroidery is complete, wash it gently in warm water and dry by pressing it in a towel.

5 Trim the fabric to the size of the coaster and insert. Snap the coaster shut.

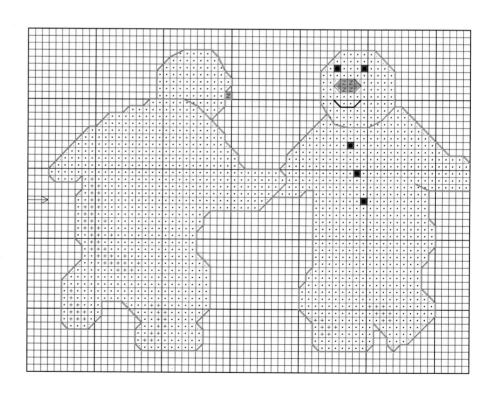

COASTER

	DMC	Anchor
• White	blanc	2
Ⓞ Dark pink	224	893
⊟ Pale pink	225	1026
◼ Black	310	403
△ Beige	612	832
Ⓩ Orange	721	324
✕ Yellow	725	305
⊞ Pale blue	775	128
▲ Brown	869	944
◿ Grey	645	273

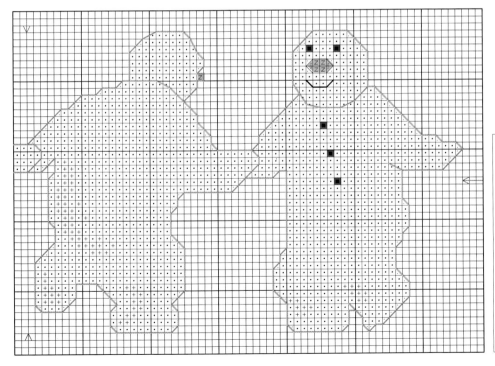

MUG

	DMC	Anchor
• White	blanc	2
◼ Black	310	403
Ⓩ Orange	721	324
⊞ Light blue	775	128
◿ Grey	645	273

Dancing Together

James's Snowman was the best dancer at the party.

This energetic design incorporates glittery threads to

give a magical effect.

You will need

- 14 count Aida in light blue,
  35 x 38cm (14 x 15in)
- Stranded embroidery thread as given in the key
- No. 24 tapestry needle
- Strong card
- Strong thread for lacing
- Mount and frame of your choice

FINISHED DESIGN SIZE

14 x 17.5cm (5½ x 7in)

STITCHING THE PANEL

1 Cut out the fabric, calculating the amount you would like to remain visible between the stitched design and the frame and leaving enough to use an embroidery frame. The amount suggested above will give approximately 5–7.5cm (2–3in) of unstitched fabric all round.

2 Prepare the fabric as instructed on page 104. Bind the edges with masking tape to prevent them from fraying. Fold your fabric in half from top to bottom, then again from left to right, and mark the centre point with a pin or thread.

3 Find the centre of the chart and mark it for your reference. Work with two strands of embroidery thread in your needle and begin stitching your design from this central point. Each cross stitch is worked across a single square of Aida. All top stitches should run in the same direction.

4 Refer to the chart and key constantly to complete the cross stitching, remembering that each square of the chart represents one stitch. Use two strands of Grey 645 to back stitch around the figures and Brown 869 for the detail on the boy's face. For The Snowman's eyes and mouth, and for the boy's dressing gown cord, back stitch with two strands of Black 310.

5 Stitch the tinsel last. The threads have a tendency to divide as you use them. This does not detract from the finished work, but adds to the glistening effect.

FINISHING THE PANEL

6 Take your finished embroidery out of the frame or hoop and hand wash it in warm water. To dry, lay it face down on a towel and press gently with a warm iron.

7 Choose a frame for the embroidery. Cut a piece of card to fit into the back of the frame and stretch the embroidery over it as explained on pages 106–7.

8 For the most dramatic effects, choose a mount in a colour that is not used much in the design, or perhaps you would like to pick a shade that complements your home furnishings. Assemble the glass (if desired), the mount and the embroidery in the frame and tape the backing board in place.

DANCING TOGETHER			
	DMC	Anchor	Madeira no. 50
⊡ White	blanc	2	
⊙ Dark pink	224	893	
⊟ Light pink	225	1026	
◼ Black	310	403	
Ⓣ Light green	470	267	
△ Beige	612	832	
⊡ Grey	645	273	
Ⓩ Orange	721	324	
⊠ Yellow	725	305	
⊞ Light blue	775	128	
Ⓘ Dark blue	809	130	
▲ Brown	869	944	
⦿ Dark green	937	268	
✳ Grey/blue tinsel			401

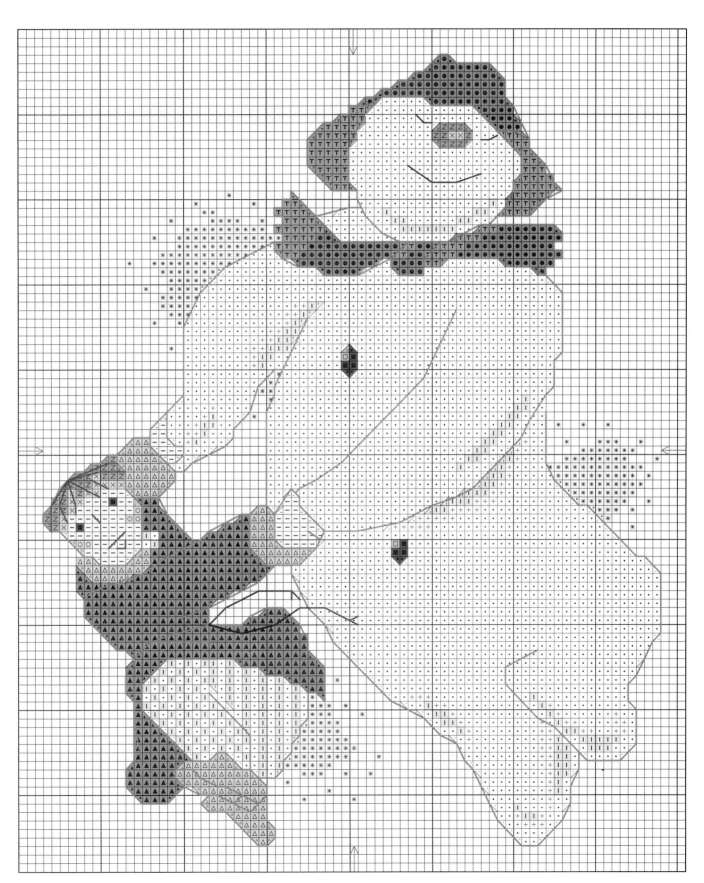

James and his Scarf

Father Christmas rummaged among the presents. "This is the one!" he beamed. It was a beautiful blue scarf. James was delighted by the gift.

You will need

- 14 count Aida in white, 38 x 35cm (15 x 14in)
- Stranded embroidery thread as given in the key
- No. 24 tapestry needle
- Strong card
- Strong thread for lacing
- Mount and frame of your choice

FINISHED DESIGN SIZE
17.5 x 14.5cm (7 x 5³/4in)

STITCHING THE PANEL

1 Cut out the fabric, deciding the amount you would like to remain visible between the stitched design and the frame. The measurements suggested will result in approximately 5–7.5cm (2–3in) of unstitched fabric all round the design.

2 Prepare the fabric as instructed on page 104. Bind the edges with masking tape to prevent them from fraying. Find the centre of your fabric and mark it with a pin or thread.

3 Find the centre of the chart and mark it for your reference. Work with two strands of embroidery thread in your needle and begin stitching your design from this central point. Work each cross stitch across one square of the fabric, making sure that the top of the stitches follow the same direction for a neat effect.

4 Refer to the chart and key constantly to complete the cross stitching, remembering that each square of the chart represents one stitch. Use two strands of Grey 645 to back stitch the outline.

5 Use Brown 869 for the detail on James's face, and Blue 809 for the fringe on the scarf, which are all in back stitch.

FINISHING THE PANEL

6 When the stitching is complete, remove your finished embroidery from the frame or hoop and hand wash it in warm water. To dry, lay the embroidery face down on a towel and press it gently with a warm iron.

7 Choose a frame for the embroidery. Cut a piece of card to fit into the back of the frame and stretch the embroidery over it as explained on pages 106–7.

8 Your mount should be in a colour that complements the embroidery. It is a good idea to pick a shade that only features slightly in the design – perhaps the grey of the outline. Alternatively, you can select a colour that reflects the décor in the room where you plan to hang your panel. Assemble the glass (if desired), the mount and the embroidery in the frame and tape the backing board in place.

JAMES AND HIS SCARF

		DMC	Anchor
·	White	blanc	2
O	Dark pink	224	893
−	Light pink	225	1026
■	Black	310	403
△	Beige	612	832
Z	Orange	721	324
X	Yellow	725	305
I	Blue	809	130
▲	Brown	869	944
◿	Grey	645	273

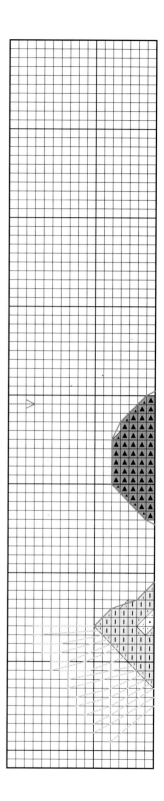

Snowy Cards

Delight your friends with these colourful Christmas cards. Choose from three attractive designs: The Snowman, James or James's house.

You *will need*

For each card:

- 14 count Aida in light blue, 20 x 15cm (8 x 6in)
- Stranded embroidery thread as given in the key
- No. 24 tapestry needle
- Greetings card, 16 x 11.5cm (6¼ x 4¼in), with an aperture of 11 x 7cm (4¼ x 2¾in)
- Double-sided sticky tape

FINISHED DESIGN SIZE

16 x 11.5cm (6¼ x 4¼in)

THE SNOWMAN CARD

1 Prepare your fabric as instructed on page 104. Use two embroidery threads throughout for the cross stitch and two threads for the back stitch.

2 Begin working at the centre of the chart and in the centre of your fabric piece. Check the colours to be used on each square. Every cross stitch is worked across a square of Aida with the top stitches going in the same direction.

3 Use Grey 645 for the back stitch around The Snowman's hat and Black 310 for The Snowman's mouth.

4 Use the metallic silver thread for the stars. It has a tendency to split, but this will enhance the sparkly effect.

STITCHING JAMES CARD

5 Prepare your fabric as instructed on page 104. Use two threads in your needle throughout the stitching of this design.

6 Starting from the centre of the pattern, complete the stitching using the colours indicated on the chart. Use Grey 645 to back stitch the outline and for James's hair. Use Black 310 for the cord of the dressing gown.

STITCHING JAMES'S COTTAGE CARD

7 Prepare the fabric as instructed on page 104. Use two embroidery threads in your needle throughout the stitching.

8 Whole cross stitch is used for the cottage and half cross stitch for the trees in the background (see page 105 for instructions). Follow the colours in the chart. Use Grey 645 for the back stitch.

FINISHING THE CARDS

9 When you have finished your stitching, hand wash your embroidery in warm water and then press it dry in a towel.

10 Cards designed to hold embroidery have three sections with an aperture cut out in the middle section. Lightly mark in pencil which of the outer sections of the card will be stuck to the back of your stitching. Place small strips of double-sided sticky tape around the edges of the aperture on the inside of the card. Then peel off the backing of the tape ready to take your design.

11 Trim the fabric so that it will overlap the aperture all round. Turn the card over and hold it above your embroidery,

making sure that the pattern is central. Press the card down onto the fabric and keep applying pressure until it holds firm.

12 Attach strips of double-sided tape around the edges of the section you marked earlier and press this down onto the section with the embroidery.

JAMES'S COTTAGE

		DMC	Anchor
·	White	blanc	2
✕	Pale yellow	744	301
+	Pale blue	775	128
I	Blue	809	130
Z	Orange	721	324
✳	Yellow	3820	306
◿	Grey	645	273
∕	*Half stitch in white*		
S	*Half stitch in blue*		

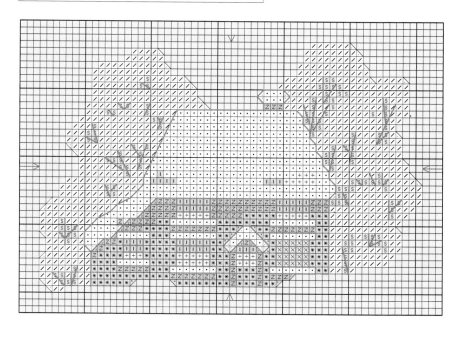

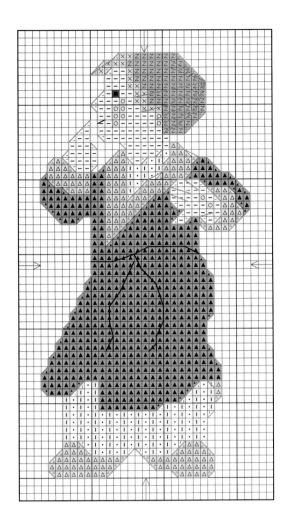

JAMES

		DMC	Anchor
·	White	blanc	2
O	Dark pink	224	893
–	Pale pink	225	1026
△	Beige	612	832
Z	Orange	721	324
X	Yellow	725	305
I	Blue	809	130
▲	Brown	869	944
◻	Black	310	403
◻	Grey	645	273

THE SNOWMAN

		DMC	Anchor
·	White	blanc	2
■	Black	310	403
T	Light green	470	267
Z	Orange	721	324
X	Yellow	725	305
+	Light blue	775	128
I	Blue	809	130
●	Dark green	937	268
◻	Grey	645	273
◻	Silver	ART281	KBF

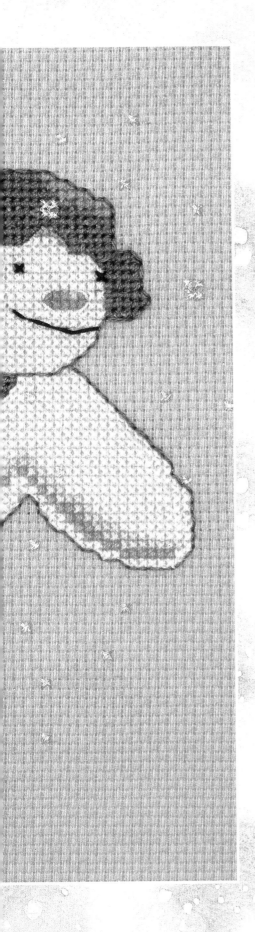

Flying Home

Once again they flew through the frosty air until they saw James's house below. This is the second flying scene, as James and The Snowman return home.

You *will* need

- 14 count Aida in light blue, 41 x 35cm (16 x 14in)
- Stranded embroidery thread as given in the key
- No. 24 tapestry needle
- Strong card
- Strong thread for lacing
- Mount and frame of your choice

FINISHED DESIGN SIZE

20 x 15.5cm (7³/4 x 6¹/4in)

STITCHING THE PANEL

1 Cut out the fabric, after deciding the amount you would like to remain visible between the stitched design and the frame. The amount suggested will give approximately 5–7.5cm (2–3in) of unstitched fabric all round the design.

2 Prepare the fabric as instructed on page 104. Bind the edges with masking tape to prevent them from fraying. Find the centre of your fabric. The easiest way is to fold it in half from top to bottom, then again from left to right, and mark the centre with a pin or thread. You will start here.

3 Find the centre of the chart and mark
it for your reference. Work with two
strands of embroidery thread in your needle
and begin stitching your design from this
central point. Work each cross stitch across
one square of the fabric. Make sure that all
top stitches run in the same direction. The
neater your stitches, the more professional
the finished design will look.

4 Refer to the chart and key constantly
to complete the cross stitching,
remembering that each square of the
chart represents one stitch. Use two strands
of Grey 645 to back stitch the outline around
the figures. Use Brown 869 for the back stitch
detail on the boy's face and hair.

FINISHING THE PANEL

5 When the stitching is complete, remove
your finished embroidery from the frame
or hoop and hand wash it in warm water.
To dry, lay the embroidery face down on
a towel and press it with a warm iron.

6 Choose a frame for the embroidery. Cut
a piece of card to fit into the back of the
frame and stretch the embroidery over it as
explained on pages 106–7.

7 When selecting the colour of your mount,
you can choose one that complements the
décor in your home, or you can pick out a
colour in the design. It is most effective to
choose colours that only feature slightly in
the design, rather than dominant ones. The
dark pink of James's glove might work well,
or the dark green of The Snowman's hat.
Assemble the glass (if desired), the mount
and the embroidery in the frame and tape
the backing board in place.

FLYING HOME		
	DMC	Anchor
⋅ White	blanc	2
⊙ Dark pink	224	893
⊟ Light pink	225	1026
■ Black	310	403
T Light green	470	267
△ Beige	612	832
▢ Grey	645	273
Z Orange	721	324
✕ Yellow	725	305
+ Light blue	775	128
I Dark blue	809	130
▲ Brown	869	·944
● Dark green	937	268
▣ Silver	ART281	KBF

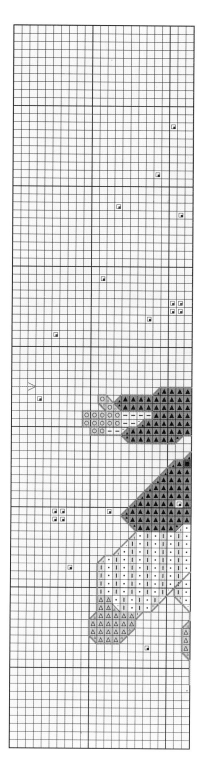

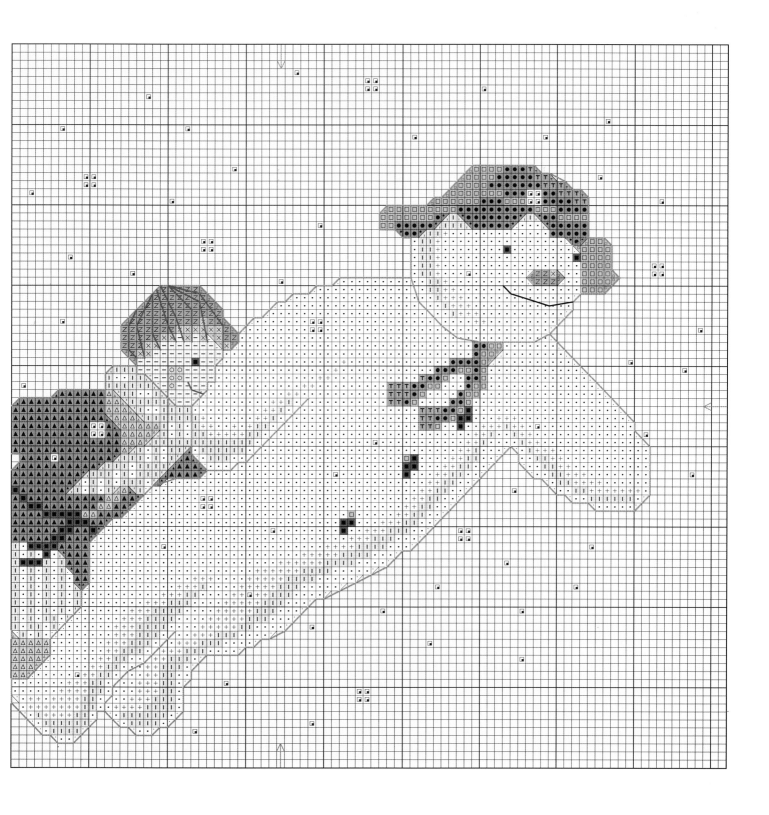

Big Hugs

James hugged The Snowman. "It's been the best Christmas ever," he whispered. Then he walked back to the house, looking over his shoulder at The Snowman.

You will need

- 14 count Aida in light blue, 30 x 41cm (12 x 16in)
- Stranded embroidery thread as given in the key
- No. 24 tapestry needle
- Strong card
- Strong thread for lacing
- Mount and frame of your choice

FINISHED DESIGN SIZE
9 x 20cm (3¹/₂ x 7³/₄in)

STITCHING THE PANEL

1 Cut out the fabric, deciding the amount you would like to remain visible between the stitched design and the frame. The measurements suggested will give approximately 5–7.5cm (2–3in) of unstitched fabric all round the design.

2 Prepare the fabric as instructed on page 104. Bind the edges with masking tape to prevent them from fraying. Fold your fabric in half from top to bottom, then again from left to right, to find the centre point; mark this with a pin or thread. You will start stitching here.

3 Find the centre of the chart and
mark it for your reference. Work with
two strands of embroidery thread in your
needle and begin stitching your design
from this central point. Work each cross
stitch across one square of the fabric.
For a neat final effect, make sure that the
top stitches run in the same direction.

4 Refer to the chart and key constantly
to complete the cross stitching,
remembering that each square of the chart
represents one stitch. Use two strands of
Grey 645 for the back stitch around the
figures. Use Brown 869 to back stitch the
boy's mouth and Black 310 for his eye.

FINISHING THE PANEL

5 When the stitching is complete, remove
your finished embroidery from the
frame or hoop. If it needs it, hand wash
your design carefully in warm water.
Then, lay the embroidery face down
on a towel and press it gently with a
warm iron until it is dry.

6 Choose a frame for your embroidery. Cut
a piece of card to fit into the back of the
frame and stretch the embroidery over it as
explained on pages 106–7.

7 The colour of your mount or frame
should co-ordinate with the colours in
the embroidery and with your home décor.
Pick out a colour that only features slightly
in the design – perhaps the yellow of James's
hair or the beige of his slippers. Assemble
the glass (if desired), the mount and the
embroidery in the frame and tape the
backing board in place.

BIG HUGS		
	DMC	**Anchor**
· White	blanc	2
O Dark pink	224	893
– Light pink	225	1026
■ Black	310	403
T Light green	470	267
△ Beige	612	832
◻ Grey	645	273
Z Orange	721	324
X Yellow	725	305
+ Light blue	775	128
I Dark blue	809	130
▲ Brown	869	944
● Dark green	937	268

Standing in his Old Place

When James looked out of his bedroom window, he saw

The Snowman standing in his old place again.

You *will need*

- 14 count Aida in light blue,
  33 x 41cm (13 x 16in)
- Stranded embroidery thread
  as given in the key
- No. 24 tapestry needle
- Strong card
- Strong thread for lacing
- Mount and frame of your choice

FINISHED SIZE

12.5 x 21.5cm (5 x 8¹/4in)

STITCHING THE PANEL

1 Cut out the fabric, deciding the amount you would like to remain visible between the stitched design and the frame. The measurements suggested will give approximately 5–7.5cm (2–3in) of unstitched fabric all round the design.

2 Prepare the fabric as instructed on page 104. Bind the edges with masking tape to prevent them from fraying. Fold the fabric in half from top to bottom, then again from left to right, and mark the centre point with a pin or thread.

3 Find the centre of the chart and mark it for your reference. Work with two strands of embroidery thread in your needle and begin stitching your design from this central point. Work each cross stitch across one square of the fabric, ensuring that the top stitches follow the same direction.

4 Refer to the chart and key constantly to complete the cross stitching, remembering that each square of the chart represents one stitch. Use two strands of Grey 645 for the back stitch around the figure of The Snowman.

5 Finish by using silver thread for the snowflakes. You may find that it splits in use, but this will just add to the sparkly effect in the night sky background.

FINISHING THE PANEL

6 Remove your finished embroidery from the frame or hoop. If it looks grubby, hand wash it carefully in warm water. To dry, lay it face down on a towel and press it gently with a warm iron.

7 Choose a frame for your embroidery. Cut a piece of card to fit into the back of the frame and stretch the embroidery over it as explained on pages 106–7.

8 Pick out a colour for your frame or mount that only features slightly in the design – perhaps the black of The Snowman's coal buttons or the dark green of his scarf. This will highlight the colour in your design. Assemble the glass (if desired), the mount and the embroidery in the frame and tape the backing board in place.

STANDING IN HIS OLD PLACE

		DMC	Anchor
·	White	blanc	2
■	Black	310	403
T	Light green	470	267
□	Grey	645	273
Z	Orange	721	324
X	Yellow	725	305
+	Light blue	775	128
I	Dark blue	809	130
●	Dark green	937	268
▣	Silver	ART281	KBF

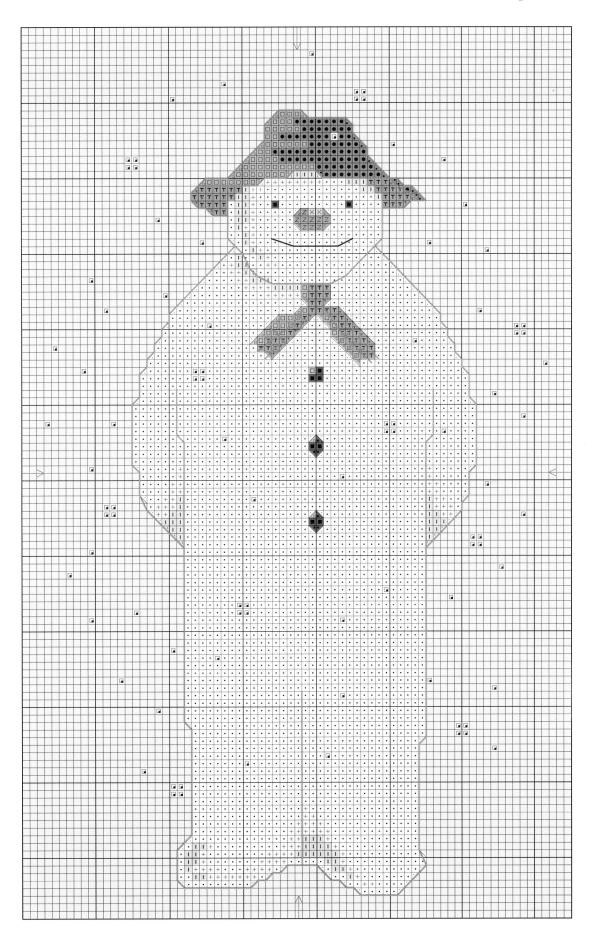

Had it All Been a Dream?

The following morning, an old hat, a scarf, some lumps

of coal and a tangerine were lying on a pile of melted snow.

Had it all been a dream? James didn't think so.....

You will need

- 14 count Aida in light blue,
  38 x 38cm (15 x 15in)
- Stranded embroidery thread as given in the key
- No. 24 tapestry needle
- Strong card
- Strong thread for lacing
- Mount and frame of your choice

FINISHED DESIGN SIZE

18.5 x 17.5cm (7¼ x 7in)

FOR THE STITCHING

1 Cut out the fabric, bearing in mind the amount you would like to remain visible between the design and the frame, and leaving enough to use an embroidery frame. The measurements suggested will leave 5–7.5cm (2–3in) of unstitched fabric.

2 Prepare the fabric as instructed on page 104. Bind the edges with masking tape to prevent them from fraying. Find the centre of your fabric then mark it with a pin or thread.

3 Find the centre of the chart and mark it for your reference. Work with two strands of embroidery thread in your needle and begin stitching your design from this central point. Work each cross stitch across one square of the fabric, ensuring that the top stitches follow the same direction. Keep your stitches as neat as you can.

4 Refer to the chart and key constantly to complete the cross stitching in the colours indicated, remembering that each square of the chart represents one stitch. Use two strands of Grey 645 to back stitch the outline and hair, and Black 310 for the backs of James's sleeves.

FINISHING THE PANEL

5 When the stitching is complete, you can remove your finished embroidery from the frame or hoop and hand wash it carefully in warm water. To dry, lay the embroidery face down on a towel and press it gently with a warm iron.

6 Choose a frame for your embroidery. Cut a piece of card to fit into the back of the frame and stretch the embroidery over it as explained on pages 106–7.

7 When choosing a colour for the mount, you can select a shade that matches the décor in the rest of your room, or one of the colours in the design. It is most effective to choose a colour that is not used much, such as the dark green or light pink. Assemble the glass (if desired), the mount and the embroidery in the frame and tape the backing board in place.

HAD IT ALL BEEN A DREAM?

		DMC	Anchor
·	White	blanc	2
O	Dark pink	224	893
−	Light pink	225	1026
■	Black	310	403
T	Light green	470	267
△	Beige	612	832
□	Grey	645	273
Z	Orange	721	324
X	Yellow	725	305
+	Pale blue	775	128
I	Blue	809	130
▲	Brown	869	944
●	Dark green	937	268

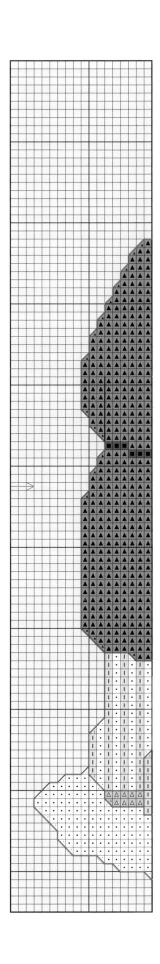

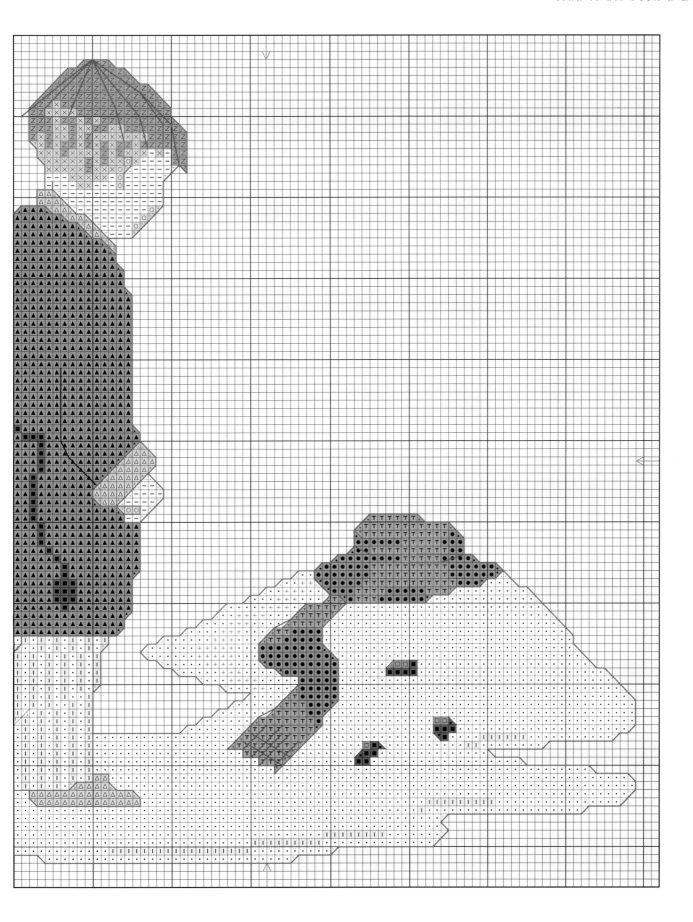

Basic Skills

The basic requirements for the designs are very simple. The colour of the fabric is consistent throughout (with two exceptions). The threads are also of similar colours for most of the designs. This means the same materials can be used for different projects, making them reasonably inexpensive to make. The stitches used throughout are simple cross stitch, half cross stitch, back stitch and straight stitch.

Each project has a chart, a full list of the materials, and guidelines on finishing and making up. A colour key for the threads is given with each chart.

It may be helpful to have the charts enlarged before you start to work to make them easier to follow. Most photocopying services will do this.

THREADS
DMC six strand threads are used throughout the book and an alternative is given for readers who prefer to use Anchor threads. Note that the Anchor colours may not be exactly the same as those used in the designs.

Cut the thread into 40cm (15in) lengths to work; longer lengths will tangle and become knotted and worn as you are working with them.

Two strands of thread are used throughout unless otherwise specified.

You will need to take care when using the metallic threads. Thread your needle in the usual way and use the thread as a double thread. The Madeira threads used in "The Christmas Tree" and "Dancing" have a tendency to split in use. This will not, however, detract from the finished design – in fact, it tends to enhance the twinkly effect. Always stitch in the metallic threads after finishing the rest of the stitching.

NEEDLES
Always use a tapestry needle for your cross stitch. These are available in several sizes but for general cross stitching, a no. 24 size is recommended. For the projects on finer Evenweave use a thinner needle, such as a no. 28 size.

FABRICS
The measurement given for the embroidery fabric includes enough excess to allow for binding the edges, working in an embroidery frame (unless specified otherwise) and mounting the finished project. Find the centre of your fabric before you begin to help you determine where to make your first stitch. To do this, first fold your fabric in half top to bottom and then fold it again from left to right. Pinch the centre point and mark it with a pin or thread.

Aida is the main fabric used in the book. The 14 count of the fabric determines the finished size of the work you are producing. If you work on a higher count, the final design will be smaller; a lower count and the design will be bigger. All fabrics have a "count" and with Aida this refers to the number of blocks or squares to 2.5cm (1in).

On the charts in this book each square corresponds with a square on the fabric. If you enlarge the charts for easier reading, remember that one square on the chart is still equivalent to one square on the fabric.

Linen is used for the table mat and napkins. This fabric is often used for cross stitching as it gives a more natural finish to the design. The stitches are usually made over two threads of linen, which tends to give a more uneven finish than with Aida, but this is usual since linen is a natural fibre.

Hardanger fabric is used for some of the small projects, such as the napkin rings. Traditionally Hardanger fabric is woven with pairs of fabric threads. The projects use 22 count or 22 threads to 2.5cm (1in) in each direction.

The coasters can be made in any evenweave fabric, count 30. Evenweave is woven of single threads and there are many available with different compositions. A cotton or cotton-synthetic mix would give a crisp result for the coaster.

STITCHING
Cross Stitch
Find the centre of your fabric before you begin. Then find the centre of the chart which is indicated by the side arrows. Do not knot your thread! Begin your

stitching by inserting your needle from the front of the fabric, holding a short length of the thread on the back of the fabric. Work the first few stitches over this length to hold it in place.

Work the first part of each stitch diagonally from one corner of the "square" to the opposite corner along a whole row in the same colour. Then work back along the same row completing the cross stitches. To make the finished cross stitching look smooth, always work the top threads in the same direction, with their points touching.

Cross stitch

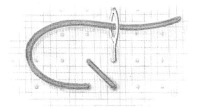

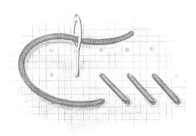

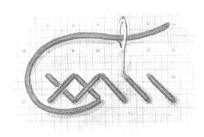

Half Cross Stitch

This stitch is the top part of the full cross stitch only and the stitches should lie in the same direction.

Three-quarter Stitch

This stitch is shown as a small symbol in the corner of a graph square.

Make a half cross stitch, and then bring your needle up through the third hole as if you were going to make a full cross stitch. Then, pass the needle through the centre of the square over the diagonal half cross stitch.

If there are two symbols in one graph square this means that two colours are required as three-quarter stitches. Do both colours as full three-quarter stitches to ensure an even distribution of colour.

Three-quarter stitch

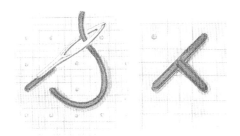

Back Stitch

This stitch is used to outline and define details in the designs. The back stitch is indicated by the lines drawn onto the charts and the colours used are explained in the instructions for each chart. Many of the back stitches differ in length. To work a line of back stitch, start by bringing the needle through to the right side of the fabric one stitch length away from the end of the line to be covered. Take the needle back through to the wrong side at the end of the stitching line, bringing it through again one stitch further along the line. The next stitch is made by returning the needle to the wrong side at the point where it emerged for the first stitch.

Back stitch

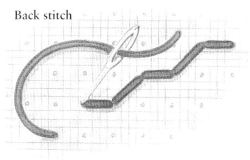

USING A FRAME

Rectangular frames are available in different sizes. The larger ones are more suitable for the larger designs, such as the panels and the cushion centre. You can use a canvas stretcher if you like, provided enough fabric is available. The edges of the fabric are simply tucked under and attached to the frame with drawing pins or staples.

To use a slate frame, cut out the fabric, allowing at least an extra 5cm (2in) all round. Oversew tape to the two side edges. Baste the vertical and horizontal centre lines on the fabric. Turn the top and bottom edges under and, working from the centre outwards using strong thread, oversew them to the roller tapes.

Fit the side pieces of the frame into the slots. Insert the pegs or adjust the screws to secure the frame. Using a large-eyed needle, secure strong thread around the intersection of the frame. Lace one of the unsecured edges of fabric to the frame, stretching the fabric evenly. Secure the thread on the intersection at the other end. Repeat this procedure to secure the final edge.

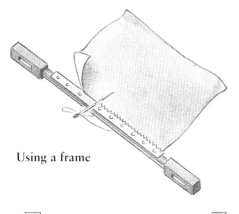

Using a frame

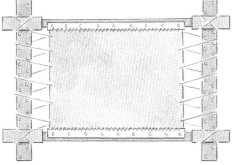

USING A HOOP

A wooden hoop, available in different sizes, is a popular frame for small designs and is used to hold the fabric stretched while you stitch. First release the tension screw on the outer ring, centre the fabric over the inner ring and press the outer ring over the top. Gently tighten the tension screw to hold the fabric firmly, ready to start work.

Using a hoop

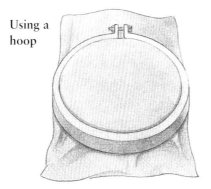

SOLVING POTENTIAL PROBLEMS
Knots

Sometimes you will find that your thread develops a knot as you work. Don't panic. It can usually be undone by sliding your needle into one of the loops of the knot to ease it loose and then gently pulling the ends of the thread to straighten it.

Unpicking

If the worst happens and you need to unpick part of your work, don't worry – it is easier than you might think. First look carefully at the chart you are working from and compare it with your

stitching to see where you have gone wrong and how much has to be redone.

Using sharp, pointed scissors, snip the top diagonal stitch to be removed. Use your needle to pull out the stitches carefully one by one. It is advisable to work in the order that the stitches were first put in. If you cannot remember this, snip the top half of one or two more stitches before trying again.

When you have removed the stitches you need to, use your needle to pull the thread ends to the wrong side of the work. Make sure there is enough to secure under the other stitches as you begin to work again.

WASHING YOUR WORK

You may need to wash the finished work. Do this using lukewarm water with a gentle fabric detergent. Rinse thoroughly, place between the folds of a towel and press most of the water out. Allow the work to dry naturally. Pad your ironing board with a clean towel and place your work face down on top. Place a clean tea towel over it and iron using a circular movement.

STRETCHING THE EMBROIDERY

You could ask a professional framer to stretch your embroidery over card before framing it, but if you wish it is not too difficult to do this for yourself.

First cut a piece of card to the size of the finished embroidery with an extra allowance so that it will fit snugly in the recess in the frame. Place the embroidery face down and centre the card on top. Fold over the top and bottom edges of the fabric and lace them together across the back of the card, using strong thread such as button thread. Repeat on the other sides, mitring the corners, and pull up the lacings tightly to stretch the fabric over the card. Overstitch the mitred corners to neaten them and check that the design is centred on the front.

Mounting embroidery with lacing

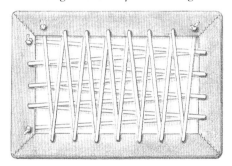

As an alternative to lacing the fabric, you could mitre the corners and secure the back with masking tape.

Mounting embroidery with masking tape

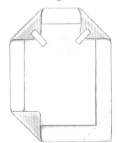 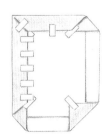

MAKING A CUSHION COVER

Sew the borders onto the embroidered fabric. Place the fabric right side down.

Fold one border strip over the other, making sure they are lying at right angles to each other, and pin. Draw a straight line on the top strip at a 45 degree angle from the inner corner to the edge. Change over the fabric strips, so that the other one is lying on top, and draw another line at a 45 degree angle. These two lines indicate where you should sew.

With the right sides together, match the lines you have drawn and pin them. Then sew the strips together. Repeat this procedure for the other three corners and trim. Press your work.

With right sides together, sew the backing fabric to the front round three

Mitred corner

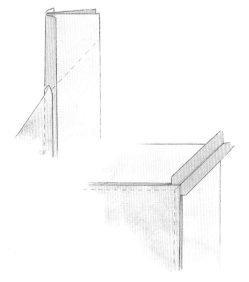

45 degree angle

sides. Insert the cushion pad and hand stitch the fourth side closed.

FINISHING TABLE LINEN

For a neat finished effect, and to prevent fraying at the edges, it is best to turn the hem edges under twice and stitch each hem by hand. Choose a thread that is the same colour as your linen.

It is best to mitre the corners. To do this, press a single hem to the wrong side of your linen. Open the hem out again and fold the corner of the fabric inwards. Refold the hem to the wrong side along the pressed line and slip stitch into place.

Hemming table linen

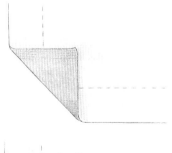

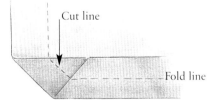

Cut line

Fold line

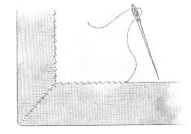

Suppliers

DMC
(Threads, Zweigart fabrics, bibs, bootees, key rings)

UK
DMC Creative World Ltd
62 Pullman Road
Wigston
Leicester
LE8 2DY
Tel: +44 (0)116 281 1040

USA
The DMC Corporation
Port Kearny Building
10 South Kearny
NJ 07032
Tel: +1 (0)973 344 0299

AUSTRALIA
DMC Needlecraft Pty Ltd
PO Box 317
Earlwood
NSW 2206
Tel: +61 (0)2 9559 3088

COATS
(Anchor threads)

UK
Coats Crafts UK
PO box 22
McMullen Road
Darlington
Co. Durham
DL1 1YQ
Tel: +44 (0)1325 394 394

USA
Coats North America
4135 South Stream Blvd
Charlotte
North Carolina 28217
Tel: +1 (0)704 329 5800

AUSTRALIA
Coats Paton Crafts
Level 1
382 Wellington Road
Mulgrave
Victoria 3170
Tel: +61 (0)39561 2288

MADEIRA
(Threads)

UK
Madeira Threads Ltd
Thirsk Industrial Park
York Road
Thirsk
North Yorks
Y07 3BX
Tel: +44 (0)1845 524 880

USA
Madeira USA
30 Bayside Court
Laconia
New Hampshire
03246 USA
Tel: +1 (0)603 528 2944

AUSTRALIA
Penguin Threads PTY Ltd
25–27 Izett Street
Pahran
Victoria 3181
Tel: +61 (0)3 9529 4400

FABRICS
Fabric Flair
Northlands Industrial Estate
Copheap Lane
Warminster
Wiltshire
BA12 0BG
Tel: +44 (0)1985 846 400

ACCESSORIES
You will find napkin rings, towels, baby accessories, key rings, mugs and all other cross stitch products at branches of Hobby Craft in the UK. In Australia and the USA, major craft stores will stock them.

Craft Creations
(**Greetings cards**)
1a Ingersoll House
Delamare Road
Cheshunt
Herts
EN8 9HD
Tel: +44 (0)1992 781900

Framecraft Ltd (**Frames**)
372–376 Summer Lane
Hockley
Birmingham
England
B19 3QA
Tel: +44 (0)121 212 0551

Acknowledgements

I would like to thank the following people for their help with producing this book: Karen Hemingway for her guidance and knowledge, Mrs Margaret Dixon for sewing samples at great speed and Harry and Stephen, members of my family, for their patience and encouragement. And with special thanks to Raymond Briggs for his inspiring creation – The Snowman.

Index

First published in 2001 by Murdoch Books UK Ltd

ISBN 1-85391-800-8

A catalogue record of this book is available from the British Library

Senior Commissioning Editor: Karen Hemingway
Project Manager: Dawn Henderson
Photo Librarian: Bobbie Leah
Editorial: Grapevine Publishing Services Ltd
Design: Maggie Aldred
Practical illustrations: Paul Bryant
Background illustrations: Nicola Gregory
Charts: Maria Diaz

CEO: Robert Oerton
Publisher: Catie Ziller
Production Manager: Lucy Byrne
International Sales Director: Kevin Lagden

Colour separation by Colourscan, Singapore
Printed by Milanostampa Italy

Murdoch Books UK Ltd
Ferry House, 51–57 Lacy Road,
Putney, London, SW15 1PR
Tel: +44 (0)20 8355 1480
Fax: +44 (0)20 8355 1499
Murdoch Books UK is a subsidiary
of Murdoch Magazines Pty Ltd.

Murdoch Books®
GPO Box 1203, Sydney,
NSW 1045, Australia
Tel: +61 (0)2 4352 7025
Fax: +61 (0)2 4352 7026
Murdoch Books® is a trademark
of Murdoch Magazines Pty Ltd.

Macmillan Distribution Ltd
Houndmills, Brunell Road
Basingstoke
Hampshire RG21 6XS
Tel: +44 (0) 1256 302707
Fax: +44 (0) 1256 351437
http://www.macmillan-mdl.co.uk